NO CHILD LEFT BEHIND ACT: TEXT, INTERPRETATION AND CHANGES

NO CHILD LEFT BEHIND ACT: TEXT, INTERPRETATION AND CHANGES

DAMIAN P. OLIVERT
EDITOR

Nova Science Publishers, Inc.
New York

For permission to use material from this book please contact us:
Telephone 631-231-7269; Fax 631-231-8175
Web Site: http://www.novapublishers.com

Library of Congress Cataloging-in-Publication Data

No Child Left Behind Act : text, interpretation, and changes / Damian P. Olivert(editor)
p. cm.
Includes bibliographical references and index
ISBN-13:978-1-59454-732-4 (hardcover)
ISBN-10: 1-59454-732-7 (hardcover)
1. United States. 3. Educational tests and measurements--Law and legislation--
United States. 4. Education--Standards--United States. 5. Educational change--United
States. I. Olivert, Damian P.
KF4195.Z9N62008
344.73'07682--dc22

2007031832

Published by Nova Science Publishers, Inc. ✢ New York

CONTENTS

Preface

On January 8, 2002, the No Child Left Behind Act of 2001, legislation to extend and revise the Elementary and Secondary Education Act (ESEA), was signed into law as P.L. 107-110 (H.R. 1). This legislation extensively amends and re-authorizes many of the programs of federal aid to elementary and secondary education. This book and accompanying CD ROM present the full text of the Act and important interpretations of it.

Chapter 1 - On January 8, 2002, the No Child Left Behind Act of 2001, legislation to extend and revise the Elementary and Secondary Education Act (ESEA), was signed into law as P.L.107-110 (H.R. 1). This legislation extensively amends and reauthorizes many of the programs of federal aid to elementary and secondary education.

Major features of the No Child Left Behind Act of 2001 include the following: (a) states will be required to implement standards-based assessments in reading and mathematics for pupils in each of grades 3-8 by the 2005-2006 school year, and at three grade levels in science by the 2007-2008 school year; (b) grants to states for assessment development are authorized; (c) all states will be required to participate in National Assessment of Educational Progress tests in 4th and 8th grade reading and mathematics every second year; (d) states must develop adequate yearly progress (AYP) standards, incorporating a goal of all pupils reaching a proficient or advanced level of achievement within 12 years, and apply them to each public school, local education agency (LEA), and the state overall; (e) a sequence of consequences, including public school choice and supplemental services options, would apply to schools and LEAs that fail to meet AYP standards for 2 or more consecutive years; (f) ESEA Title I allocation formulas are modified to increase targeting on high poverty states and LEAs and to move Puerto Rico gradually toward parity with the states; (g) within 3 years, all paraprofessionals paid with Title I funds must have completed at least 2 years of higher education or met a "rigorous standard of quality"; (h) several new programs aimed at improving reading instruction are authorized; (i) teacher programs are consolidated into a state grant authorizing a wide range of activities such as teacher recruitment, professional development, and hiring; (j) states and LEAs participating in Title I have various requirements to ensure that teachers meet the bill's definition of "highly qualified" by the end of the 2005-2006 school year; (k) almost all states and LEAs are authorized to transfer a portion of the funds they receive under several programs, and selected states and LEAs may consolidate funds under certain programs through performance agreements; (l) federal support of public school choice is expanded; (m) several previous programs are consolidated into a state grant supporting integration of technology into K-12 education; (n) the Bilingual and Emergency Immigrant Education Acts are consolidated into a single formula grant, with existing limits on the share of grants for specific instructional approaches eliminated; and (o) the 21st Century Community Learning Center program is converted into a formula grant with increased focus on after-school activities.

Chapter 2 - The No Child Left Behind Act of 2001 (NCLBA) contains several new requirements related to pupil assessments for states and local educational agencies (LEAs) participating in Elementary and Secondary Education Act (ESEA) Title I-A (Education for the Disadvantaged). These expand upon less extensive requirements that were adopted under the Improving America's Schools Act (IASA) of 1994.

Under the NCLBA, in addition to the IASA requirements for standards and assessments in reading and mathematics at three grade levels, all states participating in Title I-A will be required to implement standards-based assessments for pupils in *each* of grades 3-8 in reading and mathematics by the 2005-2006 school year. States will also have to develop and implement assessments at three grade levels in *science* by the 2007-2008 school year. Pupils who have been in U.S. schools for at least three years must be tested (for reading) in English, and states must annually assess the English language proficiency of their limited English proficient (LEP) pupils. Assessments must be of "adequate technical quality," and grants are authorized for development of enhanced assessments. Grants to states for assessment development are authorized, and $390 million has been appropriated for FY2004.

In addition, the NCLBA requires all states receiving grants under ESEA Title I-A to participate in National Assessment of Educational Progress (NAEP) tests in 4th and 8th grade reading and mathematics to be administered every two years, with all costs to be paid by the federal government. NAEP is a series of ongoing assessments of the academic performance of representative samples of pupils primarily in grades 4, 8, and 12. Beginning in 1990, NAEP has conducted a limited number of state-level assessments wherein the sample of pupils tested in each participating state is increased in order to provide reliable estimates of achievement scores for pupils in the state. Previously, all participation in state NAEP was voluntary, and additional costs associated with state NAEP were borne by participating states. The statutory provisions authorizing NAEP are amended by the NCLBA to maximize consistency with the NCLBA requirements and prohibit the use of NAEP assessments by agents of the federal government to influence state or LEA instructional programs or assessments.

Issues regarding the expanded ESEA Title I-A pupil assessment requirements, which may be addressed by the 108th Congress, include: What types of assessments will meet the ESEA Title I-A requirements? How strict will the Department of Education be in reviewing and approving state assessment systems, and will states meet the expanded assessment requirements on schedule? What will be the cost of developing and implementing the assessments, and to what extent will federal grants be available to pay for them? What might be the impact of the requirement for annual assessment of the English language proficiency of LEP pupils? What might be the impact on NAEP of requiring state participation, as well as the impact of NAEP on state standards and assessments? And what are the likely major benefits and costs of the expanded ESEA Title I-A pupil assessment requirements?

Chapter 3 - Education is one of the most important functions of government. It was a concern of the early settlers, and a focus of the Founding Fathers in writing the Constitution precisely because our democracy is dependent on an educated public. The Founders did not want education for the elite or for the many. They wanted education for all. John Adams once exclaimed: "Education for every class and rank of people down to the lowest and the poorest."

The Founding Fathers were correct: Education is necessary for the growth and prosperity of our country. As education has become more inclusive and of better quality, it has enhanced American economic and political leadership.

The task of educating the people has historically been left up to state and local governments. In the late 18th century and into the 19th century, some states, such as Virginia, Connecticut, and Pennsylvania, became known for the quality of their education systems. These school systems were the product of visionary contributions. Noah Webster worked to improve public education through writing dictionaries, spellers, readers, and histories. Benjamin Rush championed public education for girls. Horace Mann initiated efforts to improve the physical facilities of schools and to develop the first teacher training program. Thaddeus Stevens pushed through legislation I for public support of education in Pennsylvania. New York state set up the first public high schools. Other states followed, and soon public education was available for children across the country.

Recognizing the universal importance of education, the federal government assumed a larger role in financing public schools with the passage of the *Elementary and Secondary Education Act* (ESEA) in 1965. Through subsequent reauthorizations, ESEA has continued to assist the states. In 2001, the reauthorization included *No Child Left Behind,* which asks the states to set standards for student performance and teacher quality. The law establishes accountability for results and improves the inclusiveness and fairness of American education.

In: No Child Left Behind Act: Text, Interpretations and Changes ISBN 1-59454-732-7
Editor: Damian P. Olivert, pp. 1-23

Chapter 1

K-12 EDUCATION: HIGHLIGHTS OF THE NO CHILD LEFT BEHIND ACT OF 2001 (P.L. 107-110) *

Congressional Research Service Specialists and Analysts

ABSTRACT

On January 8, 2002, the No Child Left Behind Act of 2001, legislation to extend and revise the Elementary and Secondary Education Act (ESEA), was signed into law as P.L.107-110 (H.R. 1). This legislation extensively amends and reauthorizes many of the programs of federal aid to elementary and secondary education.

Major features of the No Child Left Behind Act of 2001 include the following: (a) states will be required to implement standards-based assessments in reading and mathematics for pupils in each of grades 3-8 by the 2005-2006 school year, and at three grade levels in science by the 2007-2008 school year; (b) grants to states for assessment development are authorized; (c) all states will be required to participate in National Assessment of Educational Progress tests in 4th and 8th grade reading and mathematics every second year; (d) states must develop adequate yearly progress (AYP) standards, incorporating a goal of all pupils reaching a proficient or advanced level of achievement within 12 years, and apply them to each public school, local education agency (LEA), and the state overall; (e) a sequence of consequences, including public school choice and supplemental services options, would apply to schools and LEAs that fail to meet AYP standards for 2 or more consecutive years; (f) ESEA Title I allocation formulas are modified to increase targeting on high poverty states and LEAs and to move Puerto Rico gradually toward parity with the states; (g) within 3 years, all paraprofessionals paid with Title I funds must have completed at least 2 years of higher education or met a "rigorous standard of quality"; (h) several new programs aimed at improving reading instruction are authorized; (i) teacher programs are consolidated into a state grant authorizing a wide range of activities such as teacher recruitment, professional development, and hiring; (j) states and LEAs participating in Title I have various requirements to ensure that teachers

---

*From CRS Report RL31284; January 15, 2003.

meet the bill's definition of "highly qualified" by the end of the 2005-2006 school year; (k) almost all states and LEAs are authorized to transfer a portion of the funds they receive under several programs, and selected states and LEAs may consolidate funds under certain programs through performance agreements; (l) federal support of public school choice is expanded; (m) several previous programs are consolidated into a state grant supporting integration of technology into K-12 education; (n) the Bilingual and Emergency Immigrant Education Acts are consolidated into a single formula grant, with existing limits on the share of grants for specific instructional approaches eliminated; and (o) the 21st Century Community Learning Center program is converted into a formula grant with increased focus on after-school activities.

INTRODUCTION

The No Child Left Behind Act of 2001 (NCLBA), signed into law on January 8, 2002 (H.R. 1, P.L. 107-110), extends and amends the Elementary and Secondary Education Act (ESEA). This report outlines major highlights of the NCLBA. Only the most basic provisions of this Act are briefly described in this report; other CRS reports and issue briefs have been or will be prepared or revised with more specific analyses of the major provisions of the NCLBA. In addition, several other CRS reports describe and analyze the policy debates over NCLBA provisions as they were considered during the first session of the 107th Congress.[1]

Major features of the NCLBA include the following: (a) states will be required to implement standards-based assessments in reading and mathematics for pupils in each of grades 3-8 by the 2005-2006 school year, and at three grade levels in science by the 2007-2008 school year;[2] (b) grants to states for assessment development are authorized; (c) all states will be required to participate in National Assessment of Educational Progress tests in 4th and 8th grade reading and mathematics every second year; (d) states must develop adequate yearly progress (AYP) standards, incorporating a goal of all pupils reaching a proficient or advanced level of achievement within 12 years, and apply them to each public school, local education agency(LEA), and the state overall; (e) a sequence of consequences, includingpublic school choice and supplemental services options, would apply to schools and LEAs that fail to meet AYP standards for 2 or more consecutive years; (f) ESEA Title I allocation formulas are modified to increase targeting on high poverty states and LEAs and to move Puerto Rico gradually toward parity with the states; (g) within 3 years, all paraprofessionals paid with Title I funds must have completed at least 2 years of higher education or met a "rigorous standard of quality"; (h) several new programs aimed at improving reading instruction are authorized; (i) teacher programs are consolidated into a state grant authorizing a wide range of activities such as teacher recruitment, professional development, and hiring; (j) states and LEAs participating in Title I have various requirements to ensure that teachers meet the bill's definition of "highly qualified" by the end of the 2005-2006 school year; (k) almost all states and LEAs are authorized to transfer a portion of the funds they receive under several programs, and selected states and LEAs may consolidate funds under certain programs through performance agreements; (l) federal support of public school choice is expanded; (m) several previous programs are consolidated into a state grant supporting integration of technology into K-12 education; (n) the Bilingual and Emergency Immigrant Education Acts are consolidated into a single formula grant, with existing limits on the share of grants for specific instructional approaches eliminated; and (o) the 21st Century Community Learning Center (21st CLC) program is converted into a formula grant with increased focus on after-school activities. Issues regarding implementation of many of these requirements and other provisions are likely to be considered by the 108th Congress.

Major provisions of the House- or Senate-passed versions of H.R. 1 that are *not* included in the final legislation include the Senate bill's provisions for mandatory funding at specified levels for Individuals with Disabilities Education Act (IDEA) Part B grants to states, discipline provisions for children with disabilities, authorization for up to seven states to eliminate a wide range of program requirements in return for increased accountability in terms of pupil outcomes, and pest management in schools; and the provisions in both the House- and Senate-passed versions for aggregate (i.e., not program-specific) performance bonuses or sanctions, especially for states.

Major features of the NCLBA, as well as brief references to relevant provisions of previous law, are compared in the following table.

Major Provisions of the No Child Left Behind Act of 2001 (NCLBA), P.L. 107-110 Aggregate Structure and Funding Levels of the NCLBA

Provision	Previous law	No Child Left Behind Act
Structure of the ESEA: number of programs and titles, aggregate authorization and appropriation levels, major consolidations and repeals	Prior to the NCLBA amendments, the ESEA consisted of 14 titles. In general, ESEA programs were authorized from FY1995 through FY1999, plus a 1-year automatic extension provided under the General Education Provisions Act (GEPA). In terms of funding, there were 57 line item appropriations for ESEA activities in FY2001, which totaled $18.6 billion. In addition, there were 24 ESEA activities previously authorized that were not funded in FY2001.	As amended by the NCLBA, the ESEA consists of nine titles and 45 authorizations of appropriations. Each authorization is for the period FY2002 through FY2007. For FY2002, 16 out of 45 authorizations are for such sums as may be necessary; the remaining 29 authorizations are for specific amounts that total $26.3 billion. For the period FY2003 through FY2007, all but four authorizations are for such sums as may be necessary. The four exceptions have dollar amounts specified for each year — (1) Title I, Part A Grants to LEAs; (2) Title IV, Part B 21st CCLC; (3) Title V, Part A Innovative Programs; and (4) the Fund for the Improvement of Education (FIE). For K-12 education activities outside of the ESEA, such as Education for Homeless Children and Youth or certain Indian education activities operated by the Bureau of Indian Affairs (BIA), the NCLBA includes an additional six authorizations of appropriations. The FY2002 appropriations enacted by P.L. 107-116 (Labor, Health and Human Services, Education and Related Agencies Appropriations Act) include 45 line items for ESEA activities, for a total ESEA appropriation of $21.9 billion. The 45 ESEA line items do not completely correspond with the 45 authorizations of appropriations for FY2002. Also, the single line item for the FIE includes the designation of specific appropriations for 15 separate activities, many of which were funded as separate programs in FY2001.a Major consolidations and reorganizations of ESEA authority under the NCLBA include: **(1)** Title I of ESEA, as amended by NCLBA, is expanded to include reading programs, school library programs, and programs providing dropout assistance; **(2)** Title II authorizes a broad program of teacher assistance, consolidating the former Eisenhower Professional Development and Class Size Reduction programs, plus math and science programs, and grants for technology activities; **(3)** Title III combines several bilingual education programs and emergency immigrant education assistance into a single state formula grant; **(4)** Title IV authorizes both the 21st CCLC and Safe and Drug-Free Schools and Communities Act programs (although these are retained as separate programs); **(5)** Title V includes education block grants, charter schools, magnet schools, and the FIE, which provides authority for 21 specific program-like activities; (6) Title VI authorizes state assessment grants and rural education programs; and (7) Title VII authorizes Native American programs, Title VIII remains the Impact Aid authority, and Title IX contains general provisions. With regard to major repeals, the NCLBA repeals only one K-12 program that had a sizable appropriation in FY2001 — School Repair and Renovation, first funded in FY2001 at $1.2 billion. It also repeals a number of previously unfunded programs, including the former Title XII, the School Facilities Infrastructure Improvement Act.

Assessments, Adequate Yearly Progress Standards, and Outcome Accountability Under ESEA Title I, Part A

Provision	Previous law	No Child Left Behind Act
Assessments	Assessments under ESEA Title I (which were due to be implemented in 2000-2001, although only a minority of states met this deadline) must be adopted in at least the subjects of mathematics and reading/language arts; be aligned with state content and pupil performance standards; be administered annually to students in at least one of grades 3-5, 6-9, and 10-12; include all pupils in the grades being assessed who have attended schools in the LEA for at least 1 year; involve multiple approaches; assess higher order thinking skills; and produce results disaggregated by gender, racial and ethnic groups, English proficiency status, migrant status, disability status, and economic disadvantage.	In addition to previous assessment requirements, all states participating in ESEA Title I will be required to implement standards-based assessments for pupils in *each* of grades 3-8 in reading and mathematics by the 2005-2006 school year. States will also have to develop and implement assessments at three grade levels in *science* by the 2007-2008 school year. Annual grants to states for assessment development are authorized, and states could delay administration (but not development) of the expanded assessments (above) 1 year for each year that minimum amounts are not appropriated for this purpose (the minimum is $370 million for FY2002, and P.L. 107-116 provides this amount). Pupils who have been in U.S. schools for at least 3 years must be tested (for reading) in English, and states must annually assess the English language proficiency of their limited English proficient (LEP) pupils. Assessments must be of "adequate technical quality for each purpose required under [this] Act," and grants are authorized for the development of enhanced assessments. The Department is to contract with an independent organization for a study of the assessments and accountability policies used by states to meet Title I requirements. All participating states will be required to participate in National Assessment of Educational Progress (NAEP) tests in 4th and 8th grade reading and mathematics to be administered every 2 years, with costs to be paid by the federal government. In addition, the statutory provisions authorizing NAEP are amended to maximize consistency with the NCLBA requirements, and to: provide that pupils in home schools may not be required to participate in NAEP tests; prohibit the use of NAEP assessments by agents of the federal government to influence state or LEA instructional programs or assessments; provide for review of complaints about NAEP tests; and specify that at least two members of the National Assessment Governing Board must be parents who are not employed by any educational agency
Adequate Yearly Progress (AYP) standards	States were to select AYP standards and apply these to participating LEAs and schools; there was no requirement for AYP standards for states overall. Schools and LEAs could limit the application of these standards to the specific pupils served by Title I. The previous statutory provisions regarding AYP standards were relatively broad and vague. There was no explicit requirement for a specific focus.	Previous requirements for state-developed AYP standards are substantially expanded in scope and specificity. Such standards will now have to be applied specifically to economically disadvantaged pupils, limited English proficient (LEP) pupils, pupils with disabilities, and pupils in major racial and ethnic groups, as well as all pupils, in each public school, LEA, and states overall. They will have to incorporate a goal of all pupils reaching a proficient or advanced level of achievement within 12 years. A "uniform bar" approach will be employed: states are to set a threshold percentage (of pupils at proficient or advanced levels) each year that is applicable to all pupil subgroups. The "uniform bar" must generally be increased once every 3 years, although in the initial period it must be increased after 2 years. The minimum level for the "uniform bar" in the initial period is to

Assessments, Adequate Yearly Progress Standards, and Outcome Accountability (Continued)

Provision	Previous law	No Child Left Behind Act
Adequate Yearly Progress (AYP) standards	on any high need pupil group or any specific demographic group; and no requirement that the standards incorporate a goal of all pupils reaching a proficient level of achievement by any specific future date. In practice, there was wide variation among states in the nature and apparent rigor of their standards.	be based on the greater of the percentage (of pupils at proficient or advanced levels) for the lowest-achieving pupil group or the threshold percentage for the lowest-performing quintile of schools statewide in the base year (2001-2002). Averaging of scores over 2-3 years is allowed. Under a "safe harbor" provision, a school that does not meet the standard AYP requirements may still be deemed to meet AYP if it experiences a 10% reduction in the gap between 100% and the base year for pupil groups that fail to meet the "uniform bar." For a school to meet AYP standards, 95%+ of relevant pupils must be assessed.
Outcome accountability under ESEA Title I (see also "School choice" below)	States were required to identify LEAs, and LEAs to identify schools, which failed to meet AYP standards for 2 consecutive years. Such schools and LEAs were to receive technical assistance. After the third year following identification, corrective actions — which may include loss of funds or reconstitution of school staff — were to be taken. However, most corrective actions could not be taken until standards and assessments were fully implemented, and no specific corrective action need be taken at anytime. States could reserve up to 0.5% of grants for program improvement. States were to identify especially successful "distinguished schools" and "distinguished educators," were authorized to use Title I funds reserved for program improvement to support such schools and educators. LEAs could also provide non financial rewards to these schools and educators. The Secretary of Education was authorized to reduce administrative funds to states which failed to establish standards and	While participating states are required to establish and apply AYP standards to all public schools and LEAs, a variety of actions must be taken only with respect to public schools and LEAs receiving grants under ESEA Title I-A. Schools that fail to meet AYP standards for 2 consecutive years must be identified as needing improvement; technical assistance is to be provided and public school choice must be offered to their pupils by the next school year (unless prohibited by state law). LEAs are generally required only to offer public school choice options within the same LEA; however, if all public schools in the LEA to which a child might transfer have been identified as needing improvement, then LEAs "shall, to the extent practicable," establish cooperative agreements with other LEAs to offer expanded public school choice options. If a school fails to meet the state AYP standard for 3 consecutive years, pupils from low-income families must be offered the opportunity to receive supplemental instructional services from a provider of their choice. States are to identify and provide lists of approved providers of such supplemental instructional services, which might include public or private schools, non-profit organizations, or commercial firms, and monitor the quality of the services they provide. The amount spent per child for supplemental services is to be the lesser of the actual cost of the services or the LEA's Title I-A grant per child counted in the national allocation formula (approximately $1,000 on average for FY2002).Transportation must be provided to pupils utilizing the public school choice option. LEAs are to use up to 20% of their Title I funds for transportation and supplemental services costs, although the grant to any particular school identified for corrective action or restructuring may not be reduced by more than 15%. LEAs are authorized to use Innovative Programs grants (ESEA Title V-A) to pay additional supplemental services costs. States are also authorized to use funds they reserve for program improvement or administration under Title I-A, or funds available to them under Title V-A, to pay additional supplemental services costs. If insufficient funds are available to pay the costs of supplemental services for all eligible pupils whose families wish to

Provision	Previous law	No Child Left Behind Act
Outcome accountability under ESEA Title I (see also "School choice" below)	assessments under ESEA Title I. In addition, FY2001 appropriations legislation required the provision of public school choice options, within limits, to pupils attending schools identified as needing improvement.	exercise this option, LEAs may limit services to the lowest-achieving eligible pupils. The requirement to provide supplemental services may be waived if none of the approved providers offer such services in or near a LEA. One or more of a specified series of "corrective actions" must be taken with respect to schools that fail to meet AYP for 4 consecutive years; these include replacing relevant school staff, implementing a new curriculum, decreasing management authority at the school level, appointing an outside expert to advise the school, extending the school day or year, or changing the internal organizational structure of the school. Schools that fail to meet AYP standards for 5 consecutive years must be "restructured" by implementing one or more of the following "alternative governance" actions: reopening as a charter school, replacing all or most school staff, state takeover of school operations (if permitted under state law), or other "major restructuring" of school governance. Procedures analogous to those for schools are to apply to LEAs that fail to meet AYP requirements. Both an increased state reservation (rising from 0.5%currently to 4% by FY2004) and a separate authorization of funds ($500 million for FY2002) are provided for school improvement grants. ED is required to establish a peer review process to evaluate whether states have met their statewide AYP goals. States which fail to meet their goals are to be listed in an annual report to Congress, and technical assistance is to be provided to states that fail to meet their goals for 2 consecutive years. States are to provide academic achievement awards to schools which significantly close achievement level gaps among different groups of pupils, or which exceed AYP standards for 2 or more consecutive years.
School choice	Under the ESEA, states and LEAs were authorized, but not required, to provide the option of intradistrict school choice to students attending schools that failed to meet Title I AYP requirements. Under the FY2001 appropriations legislation (P.L. 106-554), LEAs were required to offer students attending schools identified for school improvement intradistrict public school choice. Additionally, the ESEA authorized the use of Title I funds for choice programs limited to other Title I schools (although no Title I funds could	The ESEA, as amended, provides for increased public school choice opportunities by continuing or amending previous grant programs supportive of the *voluntary* provision of school choice (Innovative programs, the Public Charter Schools program, and the Magnet Schools program); and by authorizing discretionary grants under the new Voluntary Public School Choice programs. It also provides for the *mandatory* provision of public school choice in instances where schools fail to make AYP in raising the proportion of students proficient on state academic assessments. If a school fails to make AYP for 2 consecutive years, students attending that school must be offered the opportunity to transfer to a successful school in the same LEA; if the school fails for a third year, students must continue to be offered school choice and also the opportunity to receive supplemental or tutorial services. In such instances, the lowest achieving children from low-income families would receive priority. Transportation must be provided to pupils exercising public school choice options, and up to 20% of Title I-A funds may be used for such

Assessments, Adequate Yearly Progress Standards, and Outcome Accountability (Continued)

Provision	Previous law	No Child Left Behind Act
School choice	be used for transportation). The ESEA also authorized grants supportive of school choice under the Magnet Schools Assistance, Innovative Education Program Strategies, and Public Charter Schools programs.	transportation plus supplemental services. If a LEA fails to make AYP for 4 consecutive years, the state *may* require that students attending schools in that LEA be offered the opportunity to transfer to a successful school in another LEA, with transportation provided by the sending LEA. Finally, the ESEA now requires students attending persistently dangerous schools, or who be come a victim of violent crime while at school, to be allowed to transfer to a safe public school.
Reports to parents and the public regarding school system performance	Each school and LEA participating in ESEA Title I was to be reviewed annually. When standards and assessment systems were fully implemented, "individual performance profiles" were to be prepared and disseminated by LEAs for each participating school. "Statistically sound" achievement data, disaggregated by pupil gender, race or ethnicity, as well as LEP, migrant, disability, and low-income status, were to be reported for each school, LEA, and the state overall.	By the 2002-2003 school year (with a 1-year waiver authorized under exceptional or uncontrollable circumstances), pupil assessment results and certain other data for individual public schools, LEAs, and states overall must be reported to parents and the public. Report cards must generally include information on pupil performance disaggregated by race, ethnicity, and gender, as well as disability, migrant, English proficiency, and economic disadvantage status. The report cards must also include information on pupil progress toward meeting any other educational indicators included in the state's AYP standards, plus secondary school student graduation rates, the number and identity of any schools failing to meet AYP standards, and aggregate information on the qualifications of teachers. The report cards may include additional information, such as average class size or the incidence of school violence. LEA and school report cards are to be disseminated to parents of public school pupils and to the public at large. Preexisting report cards may be modified to meet these requirements.

Teacher and Paraprofessional Programs and Qualification Requirements

Provision	Previous law	No Child Left Behind Act
Teacher programs	Federal support was provided through the Eisenhower Professional Development (ESEA Title II) and Class Size Reduction (CSR — annual appropriations legislation) programs. The former was a formula grant program primarily supporting professional development for K-12 teachers. The latter was a formula grant program principally focused on reducing class sizes through the	ESEA Title II, Part A replaces the Eisenhower and CSR programs with a new state formula grant program. Authorized uses of funds are substantively expanded beyond professional development and class size reduction, and now include such activities as certification and tenure reform, merit pay, teacher testing, and training to integrate technology into the curriculum. National activities are separately authorized and include such efforts as national teacher and principal recruitment campaigns, support for advanced certification, professional development for early childhood educators, and a national panel to study teacher mobility. The NCLBA includes new provisions to shield school employees (including teachers, administrators, and school board members) from legal liability for actions taken in official capacity to maintain school discipline. In addition, teacher quality

Teacher and Paraprofessional Programs and Qualification Requirements (Continued)

Provision	Previous law	No Child Left Behind Act
Teacher programs	recruitment and hiring of new teachers.	accountability requirements are newly applied under this legislation (see below).
Teacher and paraprofessional quality requirements	Previously, the ESEA did not have specific requirements regarding teacher quality. Teacher aides/paraprofessionals hired with ESEA Title I funds generally had to have earned a high school diploma or equivalency within 2 years of being hired.	The new law requires LEAs participating in ESEA Title I, Part A to ensure that, beginning in the next school year, teachers hired with Title I, Part A funds are "highly qualified." States participating in Title I must establish plans providing that all public school teachers statewide in core academic subjects will meet the bill's definition of "highly qualified" no later than the end of the 2005-2006 school year. Further, LEAs receiving Title I Part A funds must have a plan to ensure that all teachers are highly qualified by 2005-2006. (Concern has been raised about the scope of application of this last requirement, particularly whether it applies to vocational education teachers. This issue is not yet resolved.)b Under the new law, each LEA that receives Title I-A funding must ensure that all aides or paraprofessionals *newly hired* with Title I funds after the date of enactment of P.L. 107-110 *either* must have completed at least 2 years of higher education, *or* must have both met a "rigorous standard of quality," and be able to show through a state or local academic assessment that they have knowledge of reading, writing, and math (or reading readiness, writing readiness, and math readiness) and the ability to help with instruction in these subjects. Each LEA must also ensure that, within 4 years of the date of enactment, all *existing* paraprofessionals paid with Title I funds have met those same requirements. These requirements do not apply to paraprofessionals providing translation or parental involvement services. The new law also delineates the types of responsibilities Title I paraprofessionals can undertake.
Mathematics and science education programs	The Eisenhower Professional Development program (ESEA Title II) had a funding reservation for math and science professional development.	The new law authorizes a Mathematics and Science Partnership program (ESEA Title II, Part B). Eligible partnerships that include state educational agencies, engineering, math, or science departments of higher education institutions, and high need LEAs receive funds for various activities, among them: professional development to improve math and science teachers' subject knowledge; math and science summer workshops; recruitment of math, science, or engineering majors into teaching; development of math and science curricula; and distance learning programs for math and science teachers.

Reading Programs

Provision	Previous law	No Child Left Behind Act
Reading programs	The Reading Excellence Act (REA), authorized by Title II, Part C of the ESEA, provided competitive grants to states. Authorized uses of REA funds included: professional training; providing supplemental reading support to K-3 students who needed extra help learning to read; and supporting family literacy efforts.	Reading First, authorized in Subpart 1 of ESEA Title I, Part B, replaces the REA. The Reading First program authorizes both formula grants and targeted assistance (competitive) grants to states. For FY2002 and FY2003, 100% of funds, after national reservations, will be allocated as formula grants to states, in proportion to the number of children, aged 5-17, from families with incomes below the poverty line. Beginning in FY2004, 10% of funds in excess of the FY2003 appropriation, or $90 million, whichever is less, will be reserved for targeted assistance state grants. Authorized uses of funds include: establishing scientifically based reading programs for children in grades K-3; providing reading-related professional training; providing assistance in selecting or administering screening, diagnostic, and classroom-based instructional reading assessments; providing assistance in selecting or developing effective instructional materials; strengthening coordination among schools, early literacy programs, and family literacy programs. Early Reading First, another new program authorized in Subpart 2 of ESEA Title I, Part B, is a competitive grant program with awards not to exceed 5 years. LEAs eligible for Reading First grants, and public or private organizations serving preschool-aged children, or combinations thereof, may apply for these grants. This program will fund professional training and will provide preschool-aged children with more exposure to high-quality language and literature-rich environments.
School library programs	Library services and materials has been one of several authorized uses of funds under ESEA Title VI, Part C — Local Innovative Education programs.	Improving Literacy Through School Libraries, a new program authorized in Subpart 4 of ESEA Title I, Part B, authorizes formula grants to states, in proportion to awards states receive under ESEA Title I-A, if appropriations exceed $100 million; otherwise the program will operate as a competitive grant from the Secretary of Education to eligible LEAs. Because funding for the first year, FY2002, is $12.5million, grants will be awarded competitively. Authorized uses of funds include: acquiring up-to-date school library media resources, including books; acquiring and using advanced technology; facilitating Internet links and other resource sharing networks among schools and libraries; providing professional development for school library media specialists; and providing students with access to school libraries during nonschool hours. In addition, use of funds by LEAs for library services and materials continues to be one of several authorized activities under Local Innovative Programs, now contained in ESEA Title V, Part A-3.

Special Flexibility Authorities

Provision	Previous law	No Child Left Behind Act
Special flexibility provisions	Ed-Flex (P.L. 106-25) has authorized participating states to waive a wide range of requirements for ESEA and certain other state-administered programs. ESEA Title I school wide programs have allowed many requirements under most federal programs to be waived in schools where 50% or more of pupils are from low-income families. Small, rural LEAs have been granted authority to combine funds under selected ESEA programs. Finally, the former ESEA Title XIV authorized the Secretary of Education to waive many ESEA requirements on a case-by-case basis.	In addition to previous special flexibility authorities, Title VI, Part A-1 of the revised ESEA allows most LEAs to transfer up to 50% of their grants among four programs — Teachers, Technology, Safe and Drug Free Schools, and the Innovative Programs Block Grant — or into (but not from) ESEA Title I, Part A. LEAs which have been identified as failing to meet state AYP requirements will be able to transfer only 30% of their grants under these programs, and only to activities intended to address the failure to meet AYP standards. States will be allowed to transfer up to 50% of their state activity funds among the first four of these programs plus the 21st CCLC program. Funds that are transferred must be used in accordance with all of the requirements of the program to which they are transferred. Under a State and Local Flexibility Demonstration Act (ESEA Title VI, Part A, Subpart 3), up to seven states, selected on a competitive basis, will be authorized to consolidate all of their state administration and state activity funds under the Title I-A, Reading First, Even Start, Teachers, Technology, Safe and Drug Free Schools, 21st CCLC, and Innovative Programs Block Grant programs. The consolidated funds can be used for any purpose authorized under any ESEA program. The selected states are to enter into local performance agreements with4-10 LEAs (at least one-half of which must have school-age child poverty rates of 20% or more), which may consolidate funds under the provisions of the local flexibility authority described below. In addition, participating states may specify the purposes for which all LEAs in the states use funds they receive under the ESEA Title V-A Innovative Programs block grant. This authority will be granted for a period of 5 years; states will lose the authority if they fail to meet state AYP requirements for 2 consecutive years. Further, up to 80 LEAs (no more than three per state initially), plus the LEAs which enter into agreements in states participating in the state flexibility demonstration above, will be allowed to consolidate all of their funds under the Teachers, Technology, Safe and Drug Free Schools, and Innovative Programs Block Grant programs, and to use these funds for any purpose authorized under any ESEA program. The authority will be granted for a period of 5 years; LEAs will lose the authority if they fail to meet state AYP requirements for 2consecutive years. Under both the state and local flexibility demonstration programs, several specified types of requirements — including those regarding civil rights, fiscal accountability, and private school pupil and teacher participation — may not be waived. The previous federal effort to increase funding and flexibility for small rural school districts will be continued and expanded to authorize funding for poor rural school districts (see "Rural education" section, below). The Title I-

Special Flexibility Authorities (Continued)

Provision	Previous law	No Child Left Behind Act
Special flexibility provisions		A school wide program eligibility threshold is reduced to 40%. Finally, the previous authority for the U.S. Secretary of Education to waive a variety of ESEA program requirements on a case-by-case basis is extended as Title IX, Part D.
Rural education	A Rural Education Achievement program was added to the ESEA by FY2001 appropriations legislation. This program provided eligible LEAs (rural districts with small enrollment) with flexibility in the use of funds they received under specific ESEA authorities. The program also included a 1-year authority (which was not funded) for separate grants to these LEAs.	The ESEA contains a revised Rural Education Achievement program (ESEA Title VI, Part B) that encompasses two separate programs — the Small, Rural School Achievement program, and the Rural and Low-Income School program. The first program is a revised version of the program authorized under prior law. The second program, which is new, identifies another set of districts (defined by low-income student population and rural location) and authorizes the allocation of funds to states based on the enrollment in those districts.

Education for Limited English Proficient Pupils

Provision	Previous law	No Child Left Behind Act
Education for limited English proficient (LEP) pupils	The ESEA provided competitive grants for the education of LEP pupils under the Bilingual Education Act (BEA) and formula grants for the education of recent immigrant pupils under the Emergency Immigrant Education program (EIEP). The use of BEA funds for non-bilingual instructional approaches was limited to 25% of grants. Additional assistance was authorized through Foreign Language Assistance program (FLAP) grants for two-way language programs that provide	The BEA and EIEP programs have been consolidated into a single formula grant program (if appropriations for a given fiscal year reach or exceed $650 million, as has occurred for FY2002). Grants are distributed to states based on the enrollment of LEP (80% of funds) and immigrant (20%) students. State enrollment estimates for these populations can be taken from either data available through the Bureau of the Census or data collected and submitted by SEAs, whichever the Secretary considers most accurate. No state would receive a grant less than $500,000 and the grant to Puerto Rico could not exceed 0.5% of the total available for state allotments. Continuation awards will be provided to past recipients of BEA instructional services and professional development grants. A 6.5% set-aside provides additional support for a National Professional Development Project and continued funding of the renamed National Clearinghouse for English Language Acquisition and Language Instruction programs. Within-state distribution of funds is based on the enrollment of LEP students only, regardless of students' immigrant status. However, states can reserve up to 15% for grants to eligible entities — one or more LEAs, or one or more LEAs in collaboration with an institution of higher education, a community-based organization, or a SEA — containing schools that have recently experienced large influxes of immigrant children. SEAs can reserve 5% of funds for state activities such as professional development, planning,

Education for Limited English Proficient Pupils (Continued)

Provision	Previous law	No Child Left Behind Act
Education for limited English proficient (LEP) pupils	language instruction to native English speakers and LEP pupils.	evaluation, administration, and technical assistance. The minimum grant to an eligible entity (hereafter referred to simply as an LEA) is $10,000. Participating LEAs and SEAs are subject to several accountability provisions and reporting requirements. At the end of every second fiscal year, LEAs must submit to their SEA a program evaluation that analyzes the progress made by students in the program as well as those who have moved out of the program. This evaluation must report data on the number and proportion of LEP students participating in these programs and the subsequent academic achievement of past program participants. SEAs must develop annual measurable achievement objectives that reflect: (1) the amount of time an individual child has been enrolled in a language instruction program; (2) annual increases in the number or percentage of children learning English; and (3) the number or percentage of students receiving waivers for reading or language arts assessments. Exceptions to these objectives can be made for LEAs that experience significant increases in the number of LEP and immigrant children. SEAs that find LEAs failing to meet these objectives for 2 consecutive years must provide the LEA with technical assistance to develop an improvement plan. LEAs found to be failing for 4 consecutive years can be forced to modify their language instruction program, have their funds withdrawn, and/or relevant personnel replaced by the SEA. The FLAP is extended as one of several authorized activities under the Fund for the Improvement of Education (see below).

Other ESEA Title I Provisions

Provision	Previous law	No Child Left Behind Act
Allocation of ESEA Title I-A funds to states and LEAs	In the allocation of funds to LEAs, the Title I-A statute authorized four different allocation formulas, and provided that all funds above the FY1995 level are to be allocated under the Targeted or Education Finance Incentive Grant (EFIG) formulas. However, until FY2002, appropriations acts prevented any funds from being used for these two formulas and, in practice, all funds were allocated under the Basic (84% of funds in FY2001) and Concentration (16% of funds) formulas.	In the allocation of Title I-A funds, the NCLBA provides that an amount equal to the FY2001 appropriation will be allocated under the Basic and Concentration Grant formulas, and any increases will be allocated under either an updated version of the Targeted Grant formula, or a substantially modified version of the EFIG formula. A hold harmless rate of 85%-95% of previous year grants (the higher a LEA's child poverty rate, the higher is the hold harmless percentage), previously applicable only to Basic and Targeted Grants, will now apply to each of the four Part A allocation formulas. In particular, the Concentration Grant hold harmless provision will apply to all LEAs, not just those which currently meet the eligibility criteria for this formula, except that if a LEA fails to meet such criteria for 4 successive years, then the hold harmless will no longer apply.

Other ESEA Title I Provisions (Continued)

Provision	Previous law	No Child Left Behind Act
Allocation of ESEA Title I-A funds to states and LEAs		The relative share of funds allocated to Puerto Rico will increase over time as a result of two amendments: (a) the minimum expenditure factor for Puerto Rico will be increased in stages to full parity with the minimum applicable to states (in FY2001 it was approximately 75% of the minimum for states); and (b) a cap on Targeted Grants to Puerto Rico is marginally raised. State minimum grants are increased from up to 0.25% under current law to up to 0.35%, but only with respect to appropriated funds above the FY2001 level. The NCLBA provides for the use of population data on school-age children in poor families that is updated annually, rather than, as currently, every second year, although the Census Bureau does not now publish such data, so it is not clear how or when this provision will be implemented. Major changes are made to the EFIG formula. First, in the allocation of funds to states, the population factor is changed from total school-age children to the same count of poor and other children used to calculate Basic Grants. Second, the state expenditure factor used in the other three Part A formulas would be included in the EFIG formula, although with somewhat more narrow bounds (85% and 115% of the national average rather than 80% and 120%). Third, the EFIG formula will now have a distinct intrastate allocation formula, which is based in concept on the Targeted Grant formula except that the degree of targeting will vary in three stages based on a measure of disparities in spending per pupil among each state's LEAs (the greater the disparities, the greater will be the degree of required targeting within states).
Title I migrant programs	The ESEA Title I Migrant Education program (MEP) has provided formula grants to SEAs for the development of programs targeted to migrant students. Grants have been distributed based on each states' share of migratory children enrolled in school multiplied by a state expenditure factor. Under the MEP, a migratory child has been defined as a person between the ages of 3 and 21 who is, or whose parent or spouse is, a migratory agricultural or dairy worker and who has moved from one school district (or administrative area) to another to obtain temporary or seasonal employment in the past 36 months. Children who travel more than 20 miles	The MEP remains largely unchanged from the previous reauthorization in 1994. As with Title I-A grants, the minimum expenditure factor for Puerto Rico will be increased in stages, but for this program only to 85% of the minimum applicable to states (in FY2001 it was approximately 75% of the minimum for states).

Other ESEA Title I Provisions (Continued)

Provision	Previous law	No Child Left Behind Act
Title I migrant programs	within a school district with land area larger than 15,000 square miles to engage in seasonal fishing activity may also qualify as migratory students. The enrollment estimates used in the formula are based on the number of full-time students and the full-time equivalent number of part-time students, as determined by the most accurate information available to the U.S. Secretary of Education.	
Title I neglected and delinquent programs	The ESEA Title I neglected and delinquent (N&D) program provides grants to SEAs (Subpart 1) and LEAs (Subpart 2) for educational and related services to neglected and delinquent children and youth. Formula grants are based on the number of neglected and delinquent children and youth in the state and a state expenditure factor. Local program funds may be distributed on either a formula or competitive basis to LEAs with concentrations of eligible children and youth. Local programs may serve not only youth in institutions for the delinquent or community day programs, but also youth at-risk of dropping out of school.	The N&D program remains largely unchanged from the previous reauthorization in 1994. As with Title I-A grants, the minimum expenditure factor for Puerto Rico will be increased in stages, but for this program only to 85% of the minimum applicable to states (in FY2001 it was approximately 75% of the minimum for states). The Secretary is authorized to reserve up to 2.5% of Subpart 1 funds for technical assistance and development of techniques to evaluate program effectiveness.
Comprehensive School Reform program	The Comprehensive School Reform program (CSRP) has provided grants to public elementary or secondary schools, to help pay the initial costs of implementing comprehensive strategies for educational reform. The CSRP was linked to authorizations in Title I, Section 1502, and Title X, Part A, of the ESEA, although most of the provisions governing the program were included in the FY1998 Department of Education Appropriations Act. The FY1998 appropriations legislation listed specific educational strategies	The CSRP is explicitly authorized, with relatively few substantial changes, as ESEA Title I, Part F. While only the former ESEA Title I portion of the program is explicitly authorized under the NCLBA, P.L. 107-116 provides an additional $75 million appropriation for FY2002 for CSRP grants as formerly made under ESEA Title X-A. There is no longer any explicit reference to specific school reform models; however, several characteristics which eligible comprehensive school reform models must exhibit are described (e.g., "provides high quality and continuous teacher and staff professional development"). A priority is placed on assisting schools which have failed to meet AYP standards under Title I-A. Assisted school reforms must be based on "scientifically based research and effective practices." Up to 3% of appropriations may be reserved for national quality initiatives, including public-private efforts to help

Other ESEA Title I Provisions (Continued)

Provision	Previous law	No Child Left Behind Act
Comprehensive School Reform program	which schools might seek CSRP grants to implement, although applicants could propose alternative strategies, including locally developed programs, which met specified general criteria. CSRP grants were allocated by formula to SEAs, which then selected grantee LEAs and schools on a competitive basis. Funds for the Title I portion of the CSRP were allocated to states in proportion to their Title I-A Basic Grants, while the Title X-A portion was allocated to states in proportion to their population aged 5-17. SEAs could use up to 5% of grants for administration, evaluation, and technical assistance. Grants to individual schools were to be at least $50,000 per year, renewable for up to 3 years. Schools participating in the CSRP have been supported by a series of technical assistance providers, and also have received technical support from organizations which develop and disseminate the instructional programs they adopt.	states, LEAs, and schools make informed decisions in evaluating and selecting comprehensive school reform.
Dropout programs	The previous Title V, Part C of the ESEA authorized grants to LEAs and educational partnerships for dropout prevention activities. However, no funding had been provided for this or predecessor authority since FY1995.	The newly created Dropout Prevention program, ESEA Title I-H, authorizes grants to SEAs and LEAs for activities that help prevent school dropout and encourage reentry. The procedures for allocating funds vary depending on the annual appropriation level. If appropriations are below $75 million (as is the case for FY2002), grants will be awarded competitively to SEAs and LEAs directly by ED. If appropriations exceed $75 million but are below $250 million, ED would make competitive grants to SEAs, which would then make competitive subgrants to LEAs. Finally, if appropriations exceed $250 million, grants would be made by formula to states (in proportion to Title I-A grants), with competitive subgrants to LEAs. The program targets grants to schools that serve grades 6-12 and have annual dropout rates that are above the state average as well as middle schools that feed students into such high dropout high schools. In addition, 10% of appropriations for Part H are to be used at the national level for such activities as evaluation, technical assistance, and establishment of a

Other ESEA Title I Provisions (Continued)

Provision	Previous law	No Child Left Behind Act
Dropout programs		national clearinghouse on effective practices.

Other ESEA and Related Programs

Provision	Previous law	No Child Left Behind Act
21st CCLC/After-school programs	This program was originally authorized as Part I of Title X of the ESEA. The 21st CCLC provided competitive grants to LEAs for academic and other after-school programs. Local grantees were selected directly by ED. Grant recipients could receive an award for up to 3 years and were required to include at least four out of a broad array of potential activities to serve the local community.	The program was reauthorized in ESEA Title IV, Part B. The reauthorized program is structured as a formula grant program to states, in proportion to the awards states received under Title I-A for the preceding fiscal year. SEAs must award at least 95% of their state allotment to eligible local entities (defined as LEAs, CBOs, other public or private entities, or consortia of one or more of the above) for a period of 3 to 5 years. This is a change from the program as originally authorized, which only permitted schools or consortia of schools (or LEAs operating on their behalf), to be directly awarded 21st CCLC grants. Funds may be used for before and after school activities that advance student academic achievement.
Educational technology	ESEA Title III authorized a state formula grant (Technology Literacy Challenge Fund) plus several competitive/discretionary grant programs (e.g., Technology Innovation Challenge Grants) to expand access to, and effective use of, educational technology.	The Enhancing Education Through Technology Act of 2001 (ESEA Title II, Part D) consolidates several technology programs authorized under prior law, including the Technology Innovation Challenge Grants and the Technology Literacy Challenge Fund. This new authority awards funds by formula to states and, in turn, to LEAs and eligible local entities (half of these funds are to be awarded to LEAs by formula). At least 25% of an LEA's funding must be used for professional development in the integration of advanced technologies into curricula and instruction. Other authorized activities for LEAs include increasing access to technology; using technology to connect schools and teachers with parents and students; preparing teachers to serve as technology leaders in their schools; and acquiring, expanding, implementing, repairing, and maintaining technology. State activities include distance learning, public-private initiatives for technology acquisition, and development of performance measurements to determine effectiveness of educational technology programs. Among the other technology provisions authorized in the new legislation are the following: continuation of a separate authorization for the Ready-to-Learn Television program; inclusion of the Star Schools program, Ready to Teach program (formerly Math line), and the Community Technology Centers in the Fund for the Improvement of Education (see below); and transfer of the Preparing

Other ESEA and Related Programs (Continued)

Provision	Previous law	No Child Left Behind Act
Educational technology		Tomorrow's Teachers to Use Technology to the Higher Education Act.
School safety	ESEA Title IV authorized state formula grants and competitive grants for school safety and anti-drug abuse programs.	The NCLBA amends and extends the Safe and Drug-Free Schools and Communities Act (SDFSCA) as Part A of Title IV — 21st Century Schools. State and local grants are funded for programs to prevent student violence in and around schools and the illegal use of alcohol, tobacco, and drugs. After funds reserved for outlying areas, Indian youth, and native Hawaiian youth are distributed, the remaining funds are distributed to the states by a formula of 50% based on school-age population and 50% based on ESEA Title I-A Concentration Grants for the preceding fiscal year. National programs are authorized to continue aid to recruit, hire, and train drug prevention and school safety program coordinators in schools with notable drug and violence problems. Up to $2 million is to be reserved for evaluating the national impact of the program, and funds are authorized to continue the Safe Schools/Healthy Students initiative, which is jointly funded with the Department of Health and Human Services (HHS), and the Department of Justice. Grants are permitted for LEAs and community-based groups to assist localities most directly affected by hate crimes. Funding for several new activities is authorized under national programs, such as: establishing a national center for school safety to be jointly supported by ED and the Department of Justice for emergency responses, school hotlines, consultations, and other school safety activities; providing competitive grants enabling LEAs to develop and implement programs to reduce alcohol abuse in secondary schools; and awarding grants to eligible entities to assist in creating and supporting mentoring programs for children with greatest need. Statutory provisions of the Gun Free Schools Act are incorporated into the SDFSCA requiring states to have a law to expel for 1 year any student bringing a weapon to school. In another provision of the NCLBA, a student who attends a persistently dangerous public elementary or secondary school (as determined by a state in consultation with the relevant LEA) or who becomes a victim of a violent crime (determined by state law) while on school property is allowed to transfer to a safe school, including a public charter school, within the same local school district.

Other ESEA and Related Programs (Continued)

Provision	Previous law	No Child Left Behind Act
Impact Aid	Impact Aid (ESEA Title VIII) compensates LEAs for the "substantial and continuing financial burden" resulting from federal activities. These activities include federal ownership of certain lands as well as the enrollment in LEAs of children of parents who work and/or live on federal land; for example, children of parents in the military and children living on Indian lands. Section 8007(b) authorized facilities modernization grants from 60% of funds provided for Section 8007. Eligible LEAs had to have little or no capacity to issue bonds or be defined as a 'heavily impacted' LEA under Section 8003(b)(2), and had to qualify for funds under Section 8002 (related to payments for federal ownership of land) — i.e., those with assessed property value per student below the state average, or having children living on Indian land or children of military parents comprising *at least 50%* of their total enrollment, and having a school facility emergency.	Unlike most other ESEA programs, Impact Aid had been revised and reauthorized during the 106th Congress by Title XVIII (the Impact Aid Reauthorization Act of 2000) of P.L. 106-398 (Floyd D. Spence National Defense Authorization Act for Fiscal Year 2001). P.L. 107-110 made technical changes in sections dealing with federal lands, basic support payments, and state equalization. In addition, the Act modified provisions dealing with grants to address facilities emergencies and modernization needs (under Section 8007(b) — discussed below). Finally P.L. 107-110 authorized the Act through FY2007.c Section 8007(b) was significantly modified to authorize: (a) emergency, and (b) modernization grants from 60% of funds provided for Section 8007 to qualifying LEAs (and under certain circumstances to individual schools) and sets out priorities for such grants as follows: *First*, emergency grants for LEAs with "a school facility emergency ... that poses a health or safety hazard," that are eligible for construction grant assistance under Section 8007(a), and that either have "no practical capacity to issue bonds," have "minimal capacity," or qualify for payments for certain heavily impacted LEAs. *Second*, emergency grants for LEAs with somewhat more borrowing authority and somewhat less federal impact (i.e., at least either 40% of enrollment composed of children living on Indian lands or children of parents in the military). *Third*, modernization grants for LEAs that receive Impact Aid assistance and meet either the "no capacity,"or "limited capacity" criterion or receive heavily impacted payments and have "facility needs resulting from the presence of the Federal Government, such as the enrollment of federally connected children, the presence of tax-exempt Federal property, or an increase in enrollment due to the expansion of Federal activities, housing privatization, or the acquisition of Federal property." And *fourth*, modernization grants are authorized for LEAs meeting the same criteria as those under the second priority for emergency grants (above). In addition to these eligibility requirements, a grant must be matched by local contributions and must not exceed $4 million during any 4-year period. Certain uses of grant funds are prohibited; for example, for athletic facilities.

Other ESEA and Related Programs (Continued)

Provision	Previous law	No Child Left Behind Act
Innovative programs (block grant)	Prior to the NCLBA, the Innovative Education Program Strategies program was authorized under Title VI, with many provisions similar to the new Innovative Programs authority. Formula grants are allocated to states, based on total population aged 5-17, except that no state receives less than one-half of 1% of the total. At least 85% of the state grant was required to be distributed to LEAs, using formulas developed by the states which incorporate specified general factors. The maximum state administration allocation was 25% of the 15% state-level reservation. LEA uses of funds were limited to nine targeted assistance activities.	As amended by NCLBA, ESEA Title IV, Part A, authorizes the Innovative Programs program, which is informally referred to as the "Education Block Grant." Program purposes include support of educational reform, implementation of reform and improvement programs based on scientifically based research, support of educational innovation and improvement, assistance to meet the educational needs of all students, and assistance to improve educational performance. The formula for allocating funds to states, and the provisions for state-developed formulas for allocation to LEAs, are essentially unchanged. Each state must allocate at least 85% of its grant to LEAs, except that each state must distribute to LEAs 100% of any amount received in excess of its FY2002 state grant. Remaining funds may be used at the state level to meet the purposes of this program, except no more than 15% of the remaining funds may be used for state administration. LEAs must use their grants to meet locally determined educational needs, as selected from a list of 27 innovative education assistance activities specifically authorized under the program. LEA spending must be tied to high academic achievement standards. Students enrolled in private schools are eligible to participate in the benefits of this program on an equitable basis. State applications must provide for, among other requirements, an annual report summarizing student achievement improvement.
Technical assistance	Provision of technical assistance to SEAs, LEAs, and schools by Comprehensive Regional Assistance Centers, a National Diffusion Network, Eisenhower Regional Mathematics and Science Education Consortia, and Technology-Based Technical Assistance providers was authorized under ESEA Title XIII, Parts A through D. Technology-Based Technical Assistance is not a grant program; rather, it authorized the Secretary to support the administration and implementation of ESEA. The other three programs authorized discretionary grants, and two of these programs were funded in FY2001— $28 million for Comprehensive Regional Assistance Centers, and $15 million for Eisenhower Regional Mathematics and Science	Several programs formerly authorized by ESEA are transferred without major amendment to the Educational Research, Development, Dissemination, and Improvement Act of 1994 (ERDDIA — Title IX of the P.L. 103-227). These include: Comprehensive Regional Assistance Centers (Part K of ERDDIA); National Diffusion Network (Part L); Eisenhower Regional Mathematics and Science Education Consortia (Part M); and Technology-Based Technical Assistance (Part N). A new Part J of ERDDIA, Certain Multiyear Grants and Contracts, authorizes the Secretary to continue funding for Comprehensive Regional Assistance Centers and Eisenhower Regional Mathematics and Science Education Consortia, as well as the Regional Technology in Education Consortia (formerly Section 3141 of ESEA, but not extended by NCLBA). To continue funding under Part J, these programs must have been funded through multiyear grants and contracts that were in effect the day before the enactment of the NCLBA. Authority is extended on a year-to-year basis after the multiyear grants and contracts have expired. Unlike the 6-year authorizations for ESEA programs, ERDDIA Part J authorizes such sums as may be necessary for each year, indefinitely.

Other ESEA and Related Programs (Continued)

Provision	Previous law	No Child Left Behind Act
Technical assistance	Education Consortia. In addition, the Regional Technology in Education Consortia program was funded at $10 million in FY2001. The National Diffusion Network has not been funded since FY1995.	
Education for Indians, Alaska Natives, and Native Hawaiians	Title IX of the ESEA authorized formula grants for supplemental education programs to LEAs and Bureau of Indian Affairs (BIA) funded schools, as well as discretionary grants to Native Hawaiian and Alaska Native educational organizations, and to a wider range of entities for educational improvement for Indian children and adults. The Education Amendments of 1978 (P.L. 95-561), Title XI, Part B, authorizes standards, distribution formulas, administrative grants, and other programs for BIA-funded schools. The Tribally Controlled Schools Act of 1988 (P.L. 100-297) authorizes tribes and tribal school boards operating BIA-funded schools to receive BIA grants, instead of contracts, for educational operations.	In reauthorizing Title IX of ESEA, the NCLBA renumbers it to Title VII, creates a demonstration program allowing LEAs and BIA-funded schools receiving formula grants to integrate those funds with other federal funds they receive for Indian children, and consolidates the Native Hawaiian, Alaska Native, and several additional Indian programs into fewer programs. The NCLBA reauthorizes P.L. 95-561 and P.L. 100-297, amending the former act to create a new accountability provision for BIA-funded schools, requiring that each school be accredited (or be a candidate for accreditation) within 2 years, and setting various corrective actions the Secretary of the Interior may take for schools that are still unaccredited after that time. Accreditation may be by tribal as well as regional or state accrediting agencies, as long as the tribal accreditation is acknowledged by a state or regional agency. The amendments also consolidate support services in the BIA education office, increase tribal influence in various matters, and require reports to Congress on BIA school construction needs.
Education for Homeless Children and Youth	The McKinney-Vento Homeless Assistance Act, P.L. 100-77 as amended (McKinney-Vento), authorized the Education for Homeless Children and Youth program under Subtitle B of Title VII. Formula grants were made to states in proportion to ESEA Title I-A grants to LEAs. States were required to use funds according to a state plan to ensure that homeless children and youth have access to a free, appropriate education equal to that provided to other children, and to remove existing barriers to enrollment and educational services for homeless children and youth. The previous program discouraged but did not	The NCLBA extends the Education for Homeless Children and Youth program, leaving most of the major provisions of the program in place. In particular, the key program policy states that "*homelessness alone is not sufficient reason* to separate students from the mainstream school environment." The state grant formula is based on allocations made under ESEA Title I, Part A grants to LEAs, except that no state shall receive less than the greater of (a) $150,000; (b) one-fourth of 1% of the total appropriation; and (c) the amount the state received in FY2001. Each state must allocate at least 75% of its grant to LEAs, except that it can retain up to 50% if it is funded at the minimum state grant level. With certain exceptions for health and safety emergencies, states are prohibited from using funds for either a separate school or separate program within a school. However, a "grandfather" clause allows the continuation of funding for separate schools that were in operation in FY2000 in four specified counties — San Joaquin,

Other ESEA and Related Programs (Continued)

Provision	Previous law	No Child Left Behind Act
Education for Homeless Children and Youth	prohibit the use of funds for separate schools or programs for the homeless. The statement of policy said that "... *homelessness alone should not be a sufficient reason* to separate students from the mainstream school environment ..." LEAs were required to use funds to provide services to homeless children and youth comparable to services provided to other children, and, "to the maximum extent possible," through existing programs and mechanisms that integrate homeless and nonhomeless students. States were required to distribute at least 95% of their grants to LEAs, except that they could retain at the state level up to 100% of the amount they received under the program in FY1990.	Orange, and San Diego Counties in California, and Maricopa County in Arizona. States and LEAs must assure that homeless children and youth, including unaccompanied youth, can enroll and obtain services comparable to those provided other children and youth.
Fund for Improvement of Education (FIE)	ESEA Title X-A authorized both grants for a wide variety of "nationally significant" educational activities, to be selected at the discretion of the U.S. Secretary of Education, and grants for a number of specifically authorized educational programs, such as an elementary school counseling demonstration program and a partnerships in character education pilot project. In addition, a number of grants for K-12 education activities beyond those mentioned in ESEA Title X-A have been funded under this broad authority in annual appropriations acts.	The FIE is reauthorized as ESEA Title V, Part D. This Part retains a broad authority for grants at the Secretary's discretion, as well as specific authority for support of specific educational activities in 21 Subparts, all under a single authorization of appropriations.
Prohibitions against federal control	Both the previous version of the ESEA and several other statutes — particularly the Department of Education Organization Act (DEOA) and the General Education Provisions Act (GEPA) — have prohibited federal control of numerous aspects of K-12 education policy.d	In addition to previous prohibitions against federal control of K-12 education, the NCLBA: (a) states that the federal government may not "mandate, direct, or control a State, local educational agency, or school's curriculum, program of instruction, or allocation of State or local resources, or mandate a State or any subdivision thereof to spend any funds or incur any costs not paid for under this Act;" (b) provides that ED may not "endorse, approve, or sanction any curriculum designed to be used in an elementary school or secondary school"; (c) provides that no state "shall be

Other ESEA and Related Programs (Continued)

Provision	Previous law	No Child Left Behind Act
Prohibitions against federal control		required to have academic content or student academic achievement standards approved or certified by the Federal Government, in order to receive assistance under" the ESEA; (d) prohibits the use of any ESEA funds to "develop, pilot test, field test, implement, administer, or distribute any federally sponsored national test in reading, mathematics, or any other subject, unless specifically and explicitly authorized by law"; (e) prohibits the use of any ESEA funds for any "purpose relating to a mandatory nationwide test or certification of teachers or education paraprofessionals, including any planning, development, implementation, or administration of such test or certification," and prohibits ED from "withholding funds from any State educational agency or local educational agency if the State educational agency or local educational agency fails to adopt a specific method of teacher or paraprofessional certification"; and (f) prohibits the "development of a nationwide database of personally identifiable information on individuals involved in studies or other collections of data under this Act" (other than the database on migrant children and youth authorized under the Migrant Education program, ESEA Title I-C).
Miscellaneous provisions	Not applicable	P.L. 107-110 prohibits the provision of Department of Education financial assistance to any state or local educational agency or school which "has a designated open forum or a limited public forum," and which discriminates against the Boy Scouts of America, or "any other youth group listed in Title 36 of the United States Code (as a patriotic society)," in providing equal access to school premises or facilities. At the same time, grantee agencies are not required to sponsor Boy Scout troops or other organizations affected by this provision. LEAs receiving ESEA grants must provide to armed services recruiters the same access to secondary school students as provided to postsecondary educational institutions and prospective employers.
Selected major provisions of the House- or Senate-passed versions of H.R. 1 that are *not* included in the final legislation	Not applicable	From the Senate-passed version: Mandatory funding at specified levels for Individuals with Disabilities Education Act (IDEA) Part B grants to states; discipline provisions for children with disabilities; authorization for up to seven states to eliminate a wide range of program requirements in return for increased accountability in terms of pupil outcomes; and requirements regarding pest management in schools. From both the House- and Senate-passed versions: Major performance bonuses or sanctions for *states*.

[a] For the FY2002 amounts specifically authorized for each NCLBA activity, and the FY2002 appropriations for ESEA activities, please see CRS Report RL31244, *K-12 Education*

Funding: Authorizations and Appropriations for FY2002, By Paul Irwin. [b] The definition of "highly qualified" is delineated in CRS Report RL30834, *K-12 Teacher Quality: Issues and Legislative Action*, by James B. Stedman. [c] For further information on the results of the 2000 reauthorization, the provisions regarding Impact Aid in P.L. 107-110, and an overview of the program, see CRS Report RL30075

Impact Aid: Status and Overview of 2000 Reauthorization and 2001 Amendments, by Richard N. Apling. [d] Both the DEOA and other legislation have placed explicit limits on federal control or influence. The DEOA provides that:

> *Section 103 ... The establishment of the Department of Education shall not increase the authority of the Federal Government over education or diminish the responsibility for education which is reserved to the States and local school systems and other instrumentalities of the States.*
>
> *(b) No provision of a program administered by the Secretary or by any other officer of the Department shall be construed to authorize the Secretary or any such officer to exercise any direction, supervision, or control over the curriculum, program of instruction, administration, or personnel of any educational institution, school or school system, over any accrediting agency or association or over the selection or content of library resources, textbooks, or other instructional materials by any educational institution or school system, except to the extent authorized by law.*

Almost identical provisions are contained in the GEPA. Further, parallel language prohibiting federal control of education systems was adopted in the Improving America's Schools Act (IASA, P.L. 103-382), the most recent legislation which comprehensively amended and extended the ESEA before enactment of the NCLBA. That version of the ESEA, now replaced by the NCLBA, stated that nothing in the ESEA shall be construed to authorize the federal government to "mandate, direct, or control" a state or LEA's curriculum or allocation of state and local resources, or to incur any costs not paid for by aid under ESEA programs.

All of these provisions remain in effect after enactment of the NCLBA (including the previous ESEA provision, which is continued in the revised Act).

REFERENCES

[1] For a listing of these reports, see the CRS Electronic Briefing Book, *Education (K-12)*, available at [http://www.congress.gov/brbk/html/ebedd3.html].

[2] These requirements are in addition to an ongoing, previous requirement for assessments in reading and mathematics at three grade levels.

[3] For information on the specific authorizations of appropriations in the NCLBA, and the amounts appropriated thus far for FY2002, see CRS Report RL31244, *K-12 Education Funding: FY2002 Authorizations and Appropriations for FY2002*, by Paul M. Irwin.

In: No Child Left Behind Act: Text, Interpretations and Changes ISBN 1-59454-732-7
Editor: Damian P. Olivert, pp. 27-60

Chapter 2

EDUCATIONAL TESTING: IMPLEMENTATION OF ESEA TITLE I-A REQUIREMENTS UNDER THE NO CHILD LEFT BEHIND ACT *

Wayne C. Riddle

ABSTRACT

The No Child Left Behind Act of 2001 (NCLBA) contains several new requirements related to pupil assessments for states and local educational agencies (LEAs) participating in Elementary and Secondary Education Act (ESEA) Title I-A (Education for the Disadvantaged). These expand upon less extensive requirements that were adopted under the Improving America's Schools Act (IASA) of 1994.

Under the NCLBA, in addition to the IASA requirements for standards and assessments in reading and mathematics at three grade levels, all states participating in Title I-A will be required to implement standards-based assessments for pupils in *each* of grades 3-8 in reading and mathematics by the 2005-2006 school year. States will also have to develop and implement assessments at three grade levels in *science* by the 2007-2008 school year. Pupils who have been in U.S. schools for at least three years must be tested (for reading) in English, and states must annually assess the English language proficiency of their limited English proficient (LEP) pupils. Assessments must be of "adequate technical quality," and grants are authorized for development of enhanced assessments. Grants to states for assessment development are authorized, and $390 million has been appropriated for FY2004.

In addition, the NCLBA requires all states receiving grants under ESEA Title I-A to participate in National Assessment of Educational Progress (NAEP) tests in 4th and 8th grade reading and mathematics to be administered every two years, with all costs to be paid by the federal government. NAEP is a series of ongoing assessments of the academic performance of representative samples of pupils primarily in grades 4, 8, and 12. Beginning in 1990, NAEP has conducted a limited number of state-level assessments

* From CRS Report RL31407; April 6, 2004.

wherein the sample of pupils tested in each participating state is increased in order to provide reliable estimates of achievement scores for pupils in the state. Previously, all participation in state NAEP was voluntary, and additional costs associated with state NAEP were borne by participating states. The statutory provisions authorizing NAEP are amended by the NCLBA to maximize consistency with the NCLBA requirements and prohibit the use of NAEP assessments by agents of the federal government to influence state or LEA instructional programs or assessments.

Issues regarding the expanded ESEA Title I-A pupil assessment requirements, which may be addressed by the 108th Congress, include: What types of assessments will meet the ESEA Title I-A requirements? How strict will the Department of Education be in reviewing and approving state assessment systems, and will states meet the expanded assessment requirements on schedule? What will be the cost of developing and implementing the assessments, and to what extent will federal grants be available to pay for them? What might be the impact of the requirement for annual assessment of the English language proficiency of LEP pupils? What might be the impact on NAEP of requiring state participation, as well as the impact of NAEP on state standards and assessments? And what are the likely major benefits and costs of the expanded ESEA Title I-A pupil assessment requirements?

GLOSSARY

Criterion-referenced test (CRT): "Criterion-referenced" tests measure the extent to which pupils have mastered specified content (content standard) to a predetermined degree (achievement standard). A typical criterion-referenced test result is that a 4th grade pupil's achievement in mathematics is at the "proficient" level, which is above a "basic" level, but below an "advanced" level. Most state-developed assessments, such as the Connecticut Mastery Test, the North Carolina End-of-Grade Tests, or the Texas Assessment of Academic Skills, are criterion-referenced tests.

Domain (of a test): The content and skills upon which a test is based.

Item (of a test): A test question.

Norm-referenced test (NRT): The primary distinguishing characteristic of "norm-referenced" tests is that pupil performance is measured against that of other pupils, rather than against some fixed standard of performance. Norm-referenced test results are usually expressed in terms of population percentiles along a bell-shaped distribution of tested pupils. A typical norm-referenced test result is that a 4th grade pupil's achievement in mathematics is at the 55th percentile, meaning that her or his performance is better than that of 55% of a nationally representative sample of 4th grade pupils who have taken the test under the same conditions, but worse than that of the other 45% of tested pupils in the sample. Most of the widely administered, commercially published K-12 achievement tests, such as the Iowa Test of Basic Skills, TerraNova, or the Stanford series, are norm-referenced tests, at least in their standard forms.

Standardized test: Any test for which the test items, as well as the conditions under which the test is administered, are constant. Thus, both CRTs and NRTs may be standardized tests.

INTRODUCTION

The No Child Left Behind Act of 2001 (NCLBA, P.L. 107-110), signed on January 8, 2002, contains a number of new requirements related to pupil assessments for states and local educational agencies (LEAs) participating in TitleI-A (Education for the Disadvantaged) of the Elementary and Secondary Education Act (ESEA). These new assessment requirements expand upon an earlier series of requirements for participating states to adopt curriculum content standards, academic achievement standards, and assessments linked to these at three grade levels, which were adopted under the Improving America's Schools Act (IASA) of 1994 (P.L. 103-382).

This report provides background information on state pupil assessment programs and policies, a description of the ESEA Title I-A assessment requirements as expanded by the NCLBA, a review of the implementation status of these requirements, and an analysis of related issues which may be addressed by the 108th Congress. This report will be updated occasionally, when major developments occur in the process of implementing the expanded ESEA Title I-A pupil assessment requirements.

Current State Testing Policies and Practices

The academic achievement of pupils in public elementary and secondary schools is assessed using many types of tests. Pupils may take tests developed by individual teachers or schools, commercially published tests selected by their LEA, or assessments selected and/or developed by their state educational agency (SEA). *This report will focus almost entirely on state-mandated assessments* — tests which must be administered to virtually all pupils in selected grades who attend a state's public K-12 schools — because such tests are the primary focus of federal policies regarding pupil assessment.

According to recent surveys,[1] every state except one (Iowa) now requires its LEAs to administer specified assessments to all pupils attending public schools in one or more grades.[2] The number of grades and subjects in which state-mandated assessments are administered varies widely, from only one grade and subject (e.g., the only state-mandated assessment in Nebraska currently is a writing test for pupils in grade4) to tests in multiple subjects and most K-12 grades(e.g., Alabama requires pupils in each of grades 3-11 to take state-selected tests in English, mathematics, science, and history). Few state-mandated tests are administered to pupils below grade 3, because of a variety of concerns about administering standardized tests to very young pupils, or in grade 12, in part because most assessment activity for these pupils is focused on college entrance tests. With respect to grades 3-8 in particular, 15 states plus the District of Columbia currently administer assessments in mathematics and reading to pupils in each of these grades; however, it is unclear how many of these assessments are linked to state content and achievement standards.

State-mandated assessments have been developed in one of three basic patterns. They are either: (a) developed by the states themselves, usually with technical assistance from commercial firms employing assessment specialists; (b) developed almost completely by commercial test publishers, either as generic tests sold in the same form throughout the nation,[3] or special versions of such tests which are customized to be more consistent with the curriculum content and achievement standards of a state; or (c) developed through multi-state consortia.[4]

Some state-mandated assessments, whether developed by the states themselves or in cooperation with other states or commercial firms, are "criterion-referenced" tests, or CRTs (see Glossary) designed to determine the extent to which pupils have mastered specific curriculum content and skills. Other state-mandated tests are either generic or customized "norm-referenced" tests, or NRTs (see Glossary) — tests designed primarily to rank pupils' achievement level in comparison to a nationally representative sample of pupils — purchased by states from commercial test publishers. These two types of tests vary *primarily* regarding how test results are

As of spring 2000, two states (Montana and South Dakota) administered only NRTs, 17 administered only CRTs, and 29 administered both kinds of tests in different grades and/or subject areas, with six of the latter states (Alabama, Idaho, Montana, South Dakota, West Virginia, and Wisconsin) using NRTs as their primary assessment instruments. In addition, six states (California, Delaware, Indiana, Missouri, New Mexico, and Tennessee) have developed state tests which are designed to produce *both* achievement results linked to state standards (criterion-referenced results) and nationally-normed results (norm-referenced results).

Testing Program Costs. Complete information on the costs associated with state-mandated pupil testing programs is not available. There are many potential sources of such costs, both direct and indirect, at the state, LEA, and school levels, and there are unresolved debates over how to estimate and whether to consider certain types of costs, especially indirect ones.[6]

A survey of *direct, state-level* expenditures for state-mandated assessment programs was conducted in early 2001 by the Pew Center on the States.[7] These data combine state-level expenditures for both test development and administration for FY2001 (FY2000 for North Dakota and Vermont). The figures do not include any LEA-level expenditures, either direct or indirect, nor possible indirect state level expenditures for state-mandated testing programs.

According to this survey, state-level, direct expenditures for K-12 pupil assessment programs in FY2001 totaled $422.8 million. The expenditures per state varied from zero for Iowa and $0.2 million for North Dakota, to $44.0 million for California and $26.7 million for Texas. On a per-pupil basis, these costs were found to vary from $1.46 per pupil in West Virginia to $82.55 per pupil in Alaska. Per pupil costs of state-mandated assessments tend to be low in states which rely primarily on versions of commercially-published NRTs, such as West Virginia, Alabama ($7.80 per pupil), New Mexico ($3.21 per pupil), and Utah ($3.16 per pupil). In contrast, per pupil costs were found to be highest for several states which

More detailed, but less comprehensive or current, information may be found in a study of the costs of developing and initially implementing assessments aligned with curriculum standards in two states — Kentucky and North Carolina. According to this study,[9] the total five-year state-level costs of developing and implementing a new assessment aligned with state standards for Kentucky were $9.55 million ($1.9 million per year) for test development and $33.3 million ($6.67 million per year) in total (including development, administration, etc.). For North Carolina, the total three-year state-level costs were found to be $4.0 million

($1.34 million per year) for test development and $27.5 million ($5.5 million per year) in total. The costs for these two states are not necessarily representative of the costs for all states. For example, costs might be lower for states which develop tests jointly with a group of other states, or which contract with a commercial test publisher for a customized version of a test which is marketed nationwide in a generic form.

FEDERAL POLICIES OR ACTIVITIES REGARDING PUPIL ASSESSMENTS UNDER THE NO CHILD LEFT BEHIND ACT

The following section of this report describes the major pupil assessment-related provisions of the ESEA *as amended by* the NCLBA.

ESEA Title I-A Requirements for Standards and Assessments

The provisions of ESEA Title I-A, as amended by the NCLBA, regarding standards and assessments reinforce and expand upon provisions initially adopted in the Improving America's Schools Act of 1994 (IASA). Whether under the IASA or the NCLBA, these standards and assessment provisions are linked to receipt of financial assistance under ESEA Title I-A — i.e., they apply *only* to states wishing to maintain eligibility for Title I-A grants. However, since Title I-A is the largest federal K-12 education program, funded at $11.7 billion for FY2003, it is generally considered unlikely that many states would choose not to participate in the program in order to avoid implementing the expanded assessment requirements.

The IASA of 1994 attempted to raise the instructional standards of Title I-A programs, and the academic expectations for participating pupils, by tying Title I-A instruction to state-selected curriculum content and academic achievement standards. These provisions were adopted in response to concerns that Title I-A programs had not been sufficiently challenging academically; had not been well integrated with the "regular" instructional programs of participants; and had required extensive pupil testing that was of little instructional or diagnostic value, and was not linked to the curriculum to which pupils were exposed. Further, the legislation attempted to make Title I-A tests more meaningful by using state assessments to determine whether schools and LEAs are making "adequate yearly progress" (AYP) toward meeting state achievement standards.[10]

States were given several years to meet the IASA requirements. In particular, the full system of standards and assessments was not required to be in place until the 2000-2001 school year and, as is discussed in detail below, only a minority of states met that deadline. Thus, in its debates on the NCLBA in 2001, the Congress considered not only the expanded assessment requirements proposed by the Bush Administration, but also the implementation status of requirements adopted in 1994.

Under the ESEA, as amended first by the IASA of 1994 and later by the NCLBA of 2001, states wishing to remain eligible for Title I-A grants are required to develop or adopt curriculum content standards as well as academic achievement standards and assessments tied to the standards. In general, these standards and assessments are to be applicable to all LEAs, schools, and pupils statewide. One major exception to this general policy is that if no agency or entity in a state has authority to establish statewide standards or assessments (as is the case for Iowa and possibly Nebraska), then the state may adopt either: (a) statewide standards and assessments applicable only to Title I-A pupils and programs, or (b) a policy providing that each LEA receiving Title I-A grants will adopt standards and assessments which meet the requirements of Title I-A and are applicable to all pupils served by each such LEA. Another possible exception, which is discussed further below, is that ED regulations would allow local variation in the assessments used for at least some grade levels. Thus, it should be kept in mind that "state systems of standards and assessments," as referred to frequently below, may not in some cases be uniform statewide.

In order to comply with the provisions of ESEA Title I-A, state systems of standards and assessments are required to meet a number of specific statutory requirements, as follows:

1. Standards and assessments must be developed or adopted at least in the subjects of mathematics and reading/language arts by the 2000-2001 school year.[11] Standards are to be adopted in science by the 2005-2006 school year, and assessments in science by the 2007-2008 school year.
2. The standards and assessments used to meet the Title I-A eligibility requirements must be the same as those applied to all public school pupils in the state (with the two possible exceptions discussed above).
3. The content standards are to specify what pupils are expected to know and be able to do, and are to be "coherent and rigorous."
4. Achievement standards must establish *at least* three performance levels for all pupils — advanced, proficient, and partially proficient (or basic).
5. Assessments must be aligned with state content and achievement standards.
6. Assessments in mathematics, reading and, beginning in 2007-2008, science must be administered annually to students in at least one grade in each of three grade ranges — grades 3-5, grades 6-9, and grades 10-12. In addition, assessments in mathematics and reading must be administered to pupils in *each* of grades 3-8 beginning in the 2005-2006[12] school year, if certain minimum levels of annual federal funding are provided for state assessment grants.[13]
7. All pupils in the relevant grades who have attended schools in the LEA for at least 1 year must participate in the assessments.[14]
8. LEP pupils are to be assessed in a valid and reliable manner and provided with "reasonable" accommodations. To the extent practicable, LEP pupils are to be assessed in the language and form most likely to yield accurate and reliable information on what they know and can do in academic content areas (in subjects other than English itself). However, pupils who have attended schools in the United States (excluding Puerto Rico) for 3 or more consecutive school years are to be assessed in English.[15]
9. "Reasonable" adaptations and accommodations are to be provided for students with disabilities, consistent with the provisions of the Individuals with

Disabilities Education Act (IDEA) where such adaptations or accommodations are necessary to measure the achievement of those students relative to state standards.

10. The assessment system must involve multiple approaches with up-to-date measures of student performance, including measures that assess higher order thinking skills and understanding.
11. Assessments must be used for purposes for which they are valid and reliable, and they must meet relevant, nationally recognized, professional and technical standards. In particular, the state educational agency (SEA) must provide evidence from a test publisher or other relevant source that the assessments areof adequate technical quality for the purposes required under Title I-A.
12. The assessment system must produce individual student interpretive and diagnostic reports that are provided to parents, teachers, and principals as soon as is "practically possible" after the assessments are administered. It must also enable "itemized score analyses" to be produced and reported to LEAs and schools, so that specific academic needs may be identified.
13. The assessment system must enable results for each state, LEA, and school, to be disaggregated (i.e., reported separately) by gender, major racial and ethnic groups, English proficiency status, migrant status, students with disabilities as compared to students without disabilities, and economically disadvantaged students as compared to students who are not economically disadvantaged. However, such disaggregation is not required in cases where the number of pupils in a group would be too small to yield statistically reliable information or where personally identifiable information would be revealed.
14. Assessments must objectively measure academic achievement, knowledge, and skills, and not assess personal or family beliefs and attitudes, or disclose personally identifiable information.
15. Assessment results must be provided to LEAs, schools, and teachers before the beginning of the subsequent school year.
16. In addition to the general assessment system described in 1-15 above, states are to provide that their LEAs will annually assess the English language proficiency of their LEP pupils — including pupils' oral, reading, and writing skills — beginning in the 2002-2003 school year.[16]

Finally, as is discussed further below, states receiving grants under ESEA Title I-A must participate in biennial state-level administrations of the National Assessment of Educational Progress in 4th and 8th grade reading and mathematics, beginning in the 2002-2003 school year. The timing of several of the key requirements listed above is summarized in the following table.

Schedule for Implementation of All Assessment Requirements

School Year 2000-2001

- States were to have adopted content and performance standards, plus assessments linked to these, at three grade levels in mathematics and reading. These requirements were included in the 1994 reauthorization of the ESEA. (As of the date of this report, 21 states fully met these requirements.)

School Year 2001-2002

- No new waivers of the deadlines for meeting the "1994 requirements" could be granted after April 8, 2002.

School Year 2002-2003

- States were required to begin to annually assess the English language proficiency of LEP pupils (possible one-year waiver for "exceptional or uncontrollable circumstances").
- States were first required to participate in biennial administration of NAEP.
- Annual report cards on state and LEA school systems and schools were required to be published (with a possible one year waiver authorized for "exceptional or uncontrollable circumstances").
- States were required to begin reporting annually to ED on progress toward new assessment and related requirements under the NCLBA.

May 1, 2003

- States were required to include in their ESEA consolidated application academic content standards in reading/language arts and mathematics for each of grades 3-8, as well as a detailed timeline for meeting the standard and assessment requirements listed below.

School Year 2005-2006

- Standards-based assessments in reading and mathematics must be administered to pupils in each of grades 3-8 (possible waivers if minimum amounts are not appropriated for state assessment grants or for "exceptional or uncontrollable circumstances").
- States must adopt content standards at three grade levels in science.

School Year 2007-2008

- States must begin to administer assessments at three grade levels in science.

Limits on ED Influence Over State Standards and Assessments. Several statutory constraints have been placed on the authority of the Secretary of Education in enforcing these standard and assessment requirements. First, the ESEA contains a provision — similar to others found in the Department of Education Organization Act and the General Education Provisions Act — stating that nothing in ESEA Title I shall be construed to authorize any federal official or agency to "mandate, direct, or control a State, local educational agency, or school's specific instructional content, academic achievement standards and assessments, curriculum, or program of instruction" (Section 1905[17]). Second, states may not be required to submit their standards to the U.S. Secretary of Education (Section 1111(b)(1)(A)) or to have their content or achievement standards approved or certified by the federal government (Section 9527(c)) in order to receive funds under the ESEA, other than the (limited) review necessary in order to determine whether the state meets the Title I-A requirements. Finally, no state plan may be disapproved by ED on the basis of specific content or achievement standards or assessment items or instruments (Section 1111(e)(1)(F)).

State Assessment Grants. The ESEA authorizes (in Title VI-A-1) annual grants to the states to help pay the costs of meeting the Title I-A standard and assessment requirements added by the NCLBA (i.e., the newly-required assessments in science at three grade levels and at grades 3-8 in mathematics and reading). These grants may be used by states for development of standards and assessments or, if these have been developed, for assessment administration and such related activities as developing or improving assessments of the English language proficiency of LEP pupils. The amount authorized to be appropriated for these state assessment grants, plus grants for development of enhanced assessment instruments (see below) is $490 million for FY2002 and "such sums as may be necessary" for FY2003-2007.

The state assessment requirements that were newly adopted under the NCLBA are contingent upon the appropriation of minimum annual amounts for these state assessment grants. The administration, but not the development, of grade 3-8 and science assessments may be delayed by 1 year for each year that the following minimum amounts are *not* appropriated: FY2002 — $370 million, FY2003 — $380 million, FY2004 — $390 million, and each of FY2005-2007 — $400 million. For example, if an amount less than $400 million were appropriated for state assessment grants for FY2005, the deadline for state administration of tests in reading and mathematics for each of grades 3-8 would move from 2005-2006 to 2006-2007. For FY2002 and FY2003, the minimum amounts were appropriated for these grants ($370 and $380 million, respectively). For FY2004, the minimum ($390 million) will be appropriated, assuming that the Department is able to follow through on a proposed transfer of $710,000 from a different account (i.e., the amount initially appropriated was $710,000 below the threshold).

The state assessment grants are to be allocated as follows: after reservation of 0.5% of the total for the Outlying Areas and 0.5% for the Bureau of Indian Affairs, each state will first receive $3 million. Remaining funds will be allocated among the states in proportion to their number of children and youth aged 5-17 years. This allocation formula reflects an implicit assumption that costs of assessment development are partially similar for all states, regardless of their size, and partially related to the size of the state's school age population.

The ESEA also authorizes competitive grants to states for the development of enhanced assessment instruments. Aided activities may include efforts to improve the quality, validity, and reliability of assessments beyond the levels required by Title I-A, to track student progress over time, or to develop performance or technology-based assessments. Funds appropriated each year for state assessment grants which are in excess of the "trigger" amounts for assessment development grants listed above are to be used for enhanced assessment grants; for FY2002, $17 million was available for this purpose. In February 2003, grants to nine states were announced. While each of these grants was made to a single state, each grantee has a number of "collaborators," including other states as well as, in some cases, LEAs, universities, or educational research organizations. The grants range from $1.4 to $2.3 million. The amount available for assessment enhancement grants was $4,484,000 under the FY2003 appropriation; no funds will be available for assessment enhancement grants under the FY2004 appropriation.

Finally, the NCLBA authorizes a study of the impact of the expanded Title I-A assessment requirements. The Secretary of Education is authorized to use the lesser of 15% of total appropriations for Title I, Part E (National Assessment of Title I) or $1.5 million per year to contract for an independent study of "assessments used for State accountability purposes," including the correlations between such assessments and pupil achievement, instructional practices, dropout and graduation rates, and school staff turnover rates; effects on different groups of pupils, such as LEP pupils, pupils from low-income families, or pupils with disabilities; and relationships between accountability systems and exclusion of pupils from state assessments.

National Assessment of Educational Progress[18]

The National Assessment of Educational Progress (NAEP) is a federally funded series of assessments of the academic performance of elementary and secondary students in the United States. NAEP tests generally are administered to public and private school pupils in grades 4, 8, and 12 in a variety of subjects, including reading, mathematics, science, writing and, less frequently, geography, history, civics, social studies, and the arts. NAEP assessments have been conducted since 1969.

NAEP is administered by the National Center for Education Statistics (NCES), with oversight and several aspects of policy set by the National Assessment Governing Board (NAGB), both within the U.S. Department of Education. Since 1983, the assessment has been developed primarily under a cooperative agreement with the Educational Testing Service (ETS), a private, non-profit organization which also develops and administers such assessments as the SAT. A private business firm — Westat, Inc. — carries out much of the test administration activities. Two other private firms — National Computer Systems and American Institutes for Research — distribute and score the assessments, and develop the background questionnaires, respectively.

NAEP consists of two separate groups of tests. One is the *main assessment*, in which test items (questions) are revised over time in both content and structure to reflect more current views and practices. The main assessment also reports pupil scores in relation to *performance levels* — standards for pupil achievement that are based on score thresholds set by NAGB.

The performance levels are considered to be "developmental," and are intended to place NAEP scores into context. They are based on determinations by NAGB of what pupils should know and be able to do at a basic ("partial mastery"), proficient("solid academic performance"), and advanced ("superior performance") level with respect to challenging subject matter.

The second group of NAEP tests form the long-term trend assessment, which monitors trends in math and reading achievement.[19] The tests in each subject area have not changed in content or structure since they were originally developed in 1969, making it possible to reliably compare results from year to year. However, many have expressed concerns that the long-term trend assessment questions may be increasingly disconnected from what pupils are actually taught with the passage of decades of time.[20] Since the long-term trend assessment is not involved with the ESEA Title I-A assessment requirements, it will not be discussed further.

All NAEP tests are administered to only a sample of pupils, and the tests are designed so that no pupil takes an entire NAEP test. The use of sampling is intended to minimize both the costs of NAEP and test burdens on pupils. It also makes it possible to include a broad range of items in each test. Since no individual pupil takes an entire NAEP test, it is impossible for NAEP to report individual pupil scores.[21] It is intended that NAEP tests be administered to a representative sample of all pupils in public and private schools, although there has been ongoing debate over whether LEP pupils or those with disabilities are adequately represented and whether appropriate accommodations or adaptations are being provided for them.

The frameworks for NAEP tests provide a broad outline of the content on which pupils are to be tested. Frameworks are developed by NAGB through a national consensus approach involving teachers, curriculum specialists, policymakers, business representatives, and the general public. In developing the test frameworks, national and various standards are taken into consideration, but the frameworks are

The Voluntary National Test proposal of the Clinton Administration was to develop individual versions of the NAEP 4th grade reading and 8th grade math tests (see CRS Report 97-774, *National Tests: Administration Initiative*, by Wayne Riddle). Activity related to this proposal has been terminated.

not intended to specifically reflect any particular set of standards. In addition, pupils and school staff fill out background questionnaires. The NAEP statute limits the range of background information that may be collected to data "directly related to the appraisal of academic achievement, and to the fair and accurate presentation of such information" (Section 303(b)(5)(B)) plus demographic data on pupil race, ethnicity, socioeconomic status, disability, LEP status, and gender.

State NAEP. While NAEP, as currently structured, cannot provide assessment results for individual pupils, the levels at which scores could be provided — the Nation overall, states, LEAs, or schools — depend on the size and specificity of the sample group of pupils tested. NAEP has always provided scores for the Nation as a whole and four multistate regions. Beginning in 1990, NAEP has conducted a limited number of state-level assessments in 4th and 8th grade mathematics and reading. Only the main NAEP, not the long-term trend assessment, is administered at the state level. Under state NAEP, the sample of pupils tested in a state is increased in order to provide reliable estimates of achievement scores for pupils in each participating state.

Until enactment of the NCLBA (see below), participation in NAEP was voluntary for states,[22] the additional cost associated with state NAEP administration was borne by the states and, after participating in any state NAEP test, states could separately decide whether to allow release of NAEP results for their state. As with other main NAEP tests, state NAEP scores are reported with respect to performance levels — basic, proficient, and advanced — developed by NAGB. In general, approximately 40 states participated in state-level NAEP assessments between 1990 and 2000, and all states except one (South Dakota) participated in state NAEP at least once during this period.

In addition to this administration of NAEP at a state level, FY2002 appropriations legislation provided for a Trial Urban Assessment of achievement in reading and writing — experimental administration of NAEP to expanded pupil samples in a limited number of large urban LEAs. The assessment was administered to extended samples of pupils in 2002 in Atlanta, Chicago, the District of Columbia, Houston, Los Angeles, and New York City, as part of the regular state and national assessment activities.[23]

NAEP Provisions in the No Child Left Behind Act. The NCLBA provides that all states wishing to remain eligible for grants under ESEA Title I-A will be *required* to participate in state NAEP tests in 4th and 8th grade reading and mathematics, which are to be administered every two years. The costs of testing expanded pupil samples in the states will now be paid by the federal government. An unstated, but implicit, purpose of this new requirement is to "confirm" trends in pupil achievement, as measured by state-selected assessments.[24] The results from the initial state NAEP assessment in 4th and 8th grade reading and mathematics involving all 50 states were released in November 2003.

In addition, the authorizing statute for NAEP (at that time, Sections 411-412 of the National Education Statistics Act, or NESA) was almost completely rewritten in the NCLBA. While most of the new provisions are essentially the same as previous law, the statute has been amended in several respects. It is explicitly provided that pupils in home schools may not be required to participate in NAEP tests. Agents of the federal government are prohibited from using NAEP assessments to influence state or LEA instructional programs or assessments. Mechanisms are provided for limited public access to NAEP questions and test instruments and for review of complaints about NAEP tests. Provisions regarding NAGB are revised to specify that at least two members must be parents who are not employed by any educational agency. Regarding the release of state NAEP results, participating states still may choose not to allow such release but *only* with respect to state NAEP tests *other than* those required for Title I-A purposes.

There are conflicting statutory and regulatory provisions regarding participation in NAEP tests by LEAs and schools which may be selected for NAEP test administration. The NCLBA itself explicitly provides that participation in NAEP tests is voluntary for all *pupils* and *schools*, but it contains conflicting provisions regarding voluntary participation by *LEAs*. The NAEP authorization statute (recently redesignated as Section 303 of the Education Sciences Reform Act by P.L. 107-279) states that participation is voluntary for LEAs as well, but ESEA Title I-A provides that the plans of LEAs receiving aid under that program must include an assurance that they will participate in state NAEP tests if selected (Section 1112(b)(1)(F)). Finally, program regulations published by the U.S. Department of Education (*Federal Register*, Dec. 2, 2002) require both LEAs which receive Title I-A grants, and schools within such LEAs, to participate in NAEP if selected to be among the sample tested (34 CFR 200.11(b)).

The NCLBA authorizes funds specifically for state NAEP tests for fiscal years 2002-2007 — $72 million for FY2002 and "such sums as may be necessary" for the succeeding years. The NCLBA did not extend the authorization for NAEP overall. However, TitleIII of P.L.107-279, the National Assessment of Educational Progress Authorization Act, has recently extended the general NAEP authorization through FY2008. The authorization level is $107.5 million for all NAEP activities (including state assessments), plus $4.6 million for NAGB, for FY2003, and "such sums as may be necessary" for each of FY2004-08. P.L. 107-279 also redesignates NAEP's statutory language as Title III of the Education Sciences Reform Act of 2002 (ESRA), but does not otherwise directly or substantially amend the provisions.[25]

For FY2002, the total amount appropriated for all NAEP and NAGB activities was $111.553 million. This was a large increase over the FY2001 level of $40 million, primarily as a result of the shift in responsibility for state NAEP costs from states to the federal government. The FY2002 appropriation also included $2.5 million for the Trial Urban Assessment described above. The total amount appropriated for NAEP and NAGB was $94.767 million for FY2003 and $94.763 million for FY2004.

Status of Implementation of the Assessment Requirements

The scheduled deadlines for implementation of major assessment requirements under ESEA Title I-A are outlined earlier in this report. Thus far, almost all implementation activity has taken place with respect to requirements adopted initially in the 1994 IASA and continued under the NCLBA. The process of implementing the 1994 requirements is still incomplete.

ED Review of Evidence Regarding Assessments to Meet the "1994 Requirements" Under Title I-A

In their reviews of state systems of standards and assessments, peer reviewers (specialists in the areas of standards and assessments who are not federal employees) and ED staff have been considering only various forms of "evidence" submitted by the states which are intended to document that state standards and assessments meet the specific Title I-A requirements outlined earlier in this report — i.e., they are not reviewing the assessments themselves.[26] Examples of such "evidence" include results from studies, by test publishers or others, of the degree of alignment between state standards and assessments; evaluations of the validity, reliability, or other aspects of the technical quality of state assessments; state policies on providing native language testing or other accommodations for LEP pupils, or alternate assessments or other accommodations for pupils with disabilities; provisions for reporting scores by disaggregated pupil groups; or data on the extent of actual participation in assessments of LEP pupils or pupils with disabilities.

All of the reviews conducted thus far focus primarily on the "1994 requirements" of ESEA Title I-A, because the deadlines for meeting the expanded requirements under the NCLBA have not yet occurred. However, aside from the specifics regarding grade levels and subject areas, these reviews are applicable to ESEA Title I-A as amended by the NCLBA, since the "1994 requirements" also must be met under the revised statute. In addition, these "1994 reviews" are the best currently available indication of how ED staff will implement the expanded assessment requirements as those deadlines approach.

Status of Review of State Assessment Systems with Respect to the "1994 Requirements" Under ESEA Title I-A(as of the publication date of this report)

Assessments Fully Approved (21): Colorado, Connecticut, Delaware, Indiana, Kansas, Kentucky, Louisiana, Maine, Maryland, Massachusetts, Missouri, New Hampshire, New York, North Carolina, Oregon, Pennsylvania, Rhode Island, Texas, Vermont, Virginia, Wyoming

Timeline Waiver Granted (26): Alaska, Arizona, Arkansas, California, Florida, Georgia, Hawaii, Illinois, Iowa, Michigan, Minnesota, Mississippi, Nebraska, Nevada, New Jersey, New Mexico, New York, North Dakota, Ohio, Oklahoma, Puerto Rico, South Carolina, South Dakota, Tennessee, Utah, Washington, Wisconsin

Compliance Agreement Negotiated (5): Alabama, District of Columbia, Idaho, Montana, West Virginia

As of the publication date of this report, 21 states fully met all of the pre-NCLBA requirements regarding standards and assessments (see box above). Twenty-six of the states that had not met these requirements have been granted waivers until fully meeting them within a specified period of time. These waivers have been granted under authority in Title XIV-D of the 1994 version of the ESEA or Title IX-D of the current ESEA.[27] For the remaining five states, which were found to have made the least progress toward meeting the "1994 requirements," ED has negotiated compliance agreements.[28] According to ED, "A compliance agreement allows a state to continue to receive federal education funds while it comes into compliance under specific terms, conditions, and a timeline spelled out in the written agreement, with three years as the maximum time allowed."[29]

Both before and after the NCLBA, the ESEA authorized sanctions for states failing to meet the deadlines for adopting standards and assessments. The 1994 version provided that the Secretary of Education *may* withhold funds for state administration plus program improvement from states failing to meet any of the Title I-A state plan requirements, including those related to standards and assessments (Section 1111(d)(2)). As amended by the NCLBA, the ESEA provides that the Secretary *shall* withhold 25% of funds otherwise available for state administration and program improvement activities from states which fail to meet the 1994 requirements, and *may* withhold additional state administration funds for failure to meet new assessment requirements adopted under the NCLBA. In addition, states which persistently and thoroughly fail to meet the standard and assessment requirements over an extended period of time potentially may be subject to elimination of their Title I-A grants altogether, since they would be out of compliance with a basic program requirement. In spite of these authorized or potential sanctions, no state has yet experienced any reduction in funds or other negative consequences (at least with respect to the Title I-A program specifically) due to failure to meet any deadline related to the Title I-A standard and assessment requirements.

Common Problem Areas Found in Reviews of State Assessment Systems with Respect to the "1994 Requirements". The peer reviews of state assessment systems conducted thus far have identified a number of common problem areas, as indicated in "decision letters" from ED officials to the states.[30] These are: (a) lack of adequate inclusion, accommodation, and incorporation of alternate assessments for LEP and disabled pupils; (b) insufficient documentation of the technical quality of assessments (i.e., their reliability, alignment, validity, etc.), especially the degree of alignment of assessments with content and pupil performance/achievement standards; and (c) inadequate timelines for completion and implementation of the assessments.

The first of these three problem areas has received the greatest attention. The revised ESEA, ED's "Summary Guidance on the Inclusion Requirement for Title I Final Assessments," as well as other letters and policy guidance documents, indicate that the only students who should be excluded from assessments are those who have attended public schools in a LEA for less than one year. Otherwise, *all* pupils should be included in both the assessments and associated accountability systems.[31] Where appropriate, accommodations (for example, extended time to complete an assessment) or alternate assessments[32] should be provided for pupils with disabilities.

LEP pupils should be assessed in the language most likely to yield valid results, except that those who have attended schools in the United States (other than Puerto Rico) for 3 or more years must generally be assessed in English, and they should be provided with other accommodations (e.g., extended time or use of bilingual word lists or dictionaries) where appropriate, as determined on an individual basis. With respect to inclusion of LEP pupils and those with disabilities, ED is reviewing "evidence" not only of state policies but also practices (i.e., actual rates of participation by LEP and disabled pupils). Many of the states whose assessments have not yet been approved have been informed that they need to make changes regarding assessment of or reporting of scores for LEP and/or disabled pupils.

Interpretation by ED of the Expanded Standard and Assessment Requirements of the No Child Left Behind Act

Title I-A Standard and Assessment Requirements. On July 5, 2002, ED published regulations on the Title I-A assessment requirements newly adopted under the NCLBA.[33] Under the provisions of ESEA Title I, Part I, ED was required to establish a "negotiated rulemaking" procedure, as authorized under the Negotiated Rulemaking Act of 1990, in developing regulations regarding the Title I-A standards and assessments requirements.

Under negotiated rulemaking, ED solicits advice from "representatives of Federal, State, and local administrators, parents, teachers, paraprofessionals, and members of local school boards or other organizations involved with the implementation and operation of" Title I-A programs (Section 1901(b)(1)), after which an initial draft of proposed regulations is prepared. ED selects representatives of these organizations to participate in a negotiated rulemaking process, to include persons "from all geographic regions of the United States, in such numbers as will provide an equitable balance between representatives of parents and students and representatives of educators and education officials" (Section 1901(b)(3)(B)).

The selected representatives are to discuss the Department's draft of proposed regulations, and make any changes to this, consistent with the authorizing statute, on which they can reach consensus. The NCLBA provides that "published proposed regulations shall conform to agreements that result from negotiated rulemaking" *unless* "the Secretary reopens the negotiated rulemaking process or provides a written explanation to the participants involved in the process explaining why the Secretary decided to depart from, and not adhere to, such agreements" (ESEA Title I, Section 1902(a)). Thus, ED is encouraged, but not required, to follow the recommendations of the negotiated rulemaking panel, and the process may be viewed primarily as an additional mechanism, beyond publication for comments in the *Federal Register*, of obtaining input on proposed regulations from concerned organizations.[34]

Significant features of the Department's final regulations — developed through the negotiated rulemaking process[35] and published in the *Federal Register* on July 5, 2002 — are described below. In general, the regulations repeat statutory requirements, while clarifying the following points: (a) content standards can cover multiple grades, but they must include grade-specific "content expectations," and achievement standards must be grade-specific; (b) high school standards must cover what *all* high school students are expected to know and be able to do; (c) assessments may include extended or essay response items or ask a pupil to analyze text or express opinions; (d) assessments may include either CRTs or NRTs, although any NRTs used must be augmented to "measure accurately the depth and breadth of" the state's content standards, provide results expressed in terms of the state's achievement standards, and be "designed to provide a coherent system across grades and subjects;" (e) state assessment systems may include assessments which vary by LEA in some grades,[36] and any LEA-selected assessments used to meet the Title I-A requirements must be "equivalent to one another and to state assessments, where they exist, in their content coverage, difficulty, and quality," "have comparable validity and reliability," provide "consistent determinations of the annual progress of schools and LEAs within the state," and produce results which are sufficiently comparable that they can be aggregated; (f) LEP, migrant, and homeless pupils are to be included in the assessment system at all times; (g) states are to determine the minimum number of students from specific demographic groups to include in public reports or accountability calculations, to maintain statistical reliability and protect privacy; (h) the requirement for dissemination of "itemized score analyses" does not require the release of individual test items; (i) states must provide evidence, from test publishers or other "relevant sources," that their assessment systems are of adequate technical quality to meet each purpose required under Title I-A, and this information can be made available by ED to the public, consistent with applicable federal laws on disclosure of information; (j) the assessment requirements apply only to public schools and their pupils, not to private (or home) schools, although the achievement of private school pupils who participate in Title I-A must be assessed in *some* manner; (k) while states must develop achievement (as well as content) standards in science by 2005-2006, they need not develop specific cut scores for the achievement levels until 2007-2008, when the assessments must be implemented; and (l) for purposes of disaggregated score reporting, "pupils with disabilities" are only those identified under the IDEA,[37] although all pupils with disabilities, whether identified under the IDEA or Section 504 of the Rehabilitation Act, are to be included in assessments and provided with appropriate accommodations.

Recent ED Policy Developments Regarding Participation Rates Plus Treatment of Limited English Proficient Pupils and Certain Pupils With Disabilities in Assessments and AYP Determinations. ED officials have recently published regulations and other policy guidance on participation rates plus the treatment of limited English proficient pupils and certain pupils with disabilities in assessments and the calculation of AYP for schools and LEAs, in an effort to provide additional flexibility and reduce the number of schools and LEAs identified as failing to make AYP. On March 29, 2004, ED announced that schools could meet the requirement that 95% or more of pupils (all pupils as well as pupils in each designated demographic group) participate in assessments (in order for the school or LEA to make AYP) on the basis of *average* participation rates for the last two or three years, rather than having to post a 95% or higher participation rate each year. In other words, if a particular demographic group of pupils in a school has a 93% test participation rate in the most recent year, but had a 97% rate the preceding year, the 95% participation rate requirement would be met. In addition, the new guidance would allow schools to exclude pupils who fail to participate in assessments due to a "significant medical emergency" from the participation rate calculations. The new guidance further emphasizes the authority for states to allow pupils who miss a primary assessment date to take make-up tests, and to determine the minimum size for demographic groups of pupils to be considered in making AYP determinations (including those related to participation rates). According to ED, in some states, as many as 20% of the schools failing to make AYP did so on the basis of assessment participation rates alone. It is not known how many of these schools would meet the new, somewhat more relaxed standard.

On February 19, 2004, ED officials announced two new policies with respect to LEP pupils.[38] First, with respect to assessments, LEP pupils in their *first year* of attending schools in the United States must participate in English language proficiency and mathematics tests. However, the participation of such pupils in

reading tests, as well as the inclusion of these pupils' test scores in AYP calculations, is to be optional (i.e., schools and LEAs need not consider the scores of first year LEP pupils in determining whether schools or LEAs meet AYP standards). Second, in AYP determinations, schools and LEAs may continue to include pupils in the LEP demographic category for up to two years after they have attained proficiency in English. Both these options, if exercised, should increase average test scores for LEP pupil groups, and reduce the extent to which schools or LEAs fail to meet AYP on the basis of such pupils.

Additional regulations, addressing the application of the Title I-A standard and assessment requirements to certain pupils with disabilities, were published in the *Federal Register* on December 9, 2003 (pp. 68698-68708). These regulations amend the regulations published on July 5, 2002, discussed above, as well as final regulations on other aspects of Title I-A accountability requirements, published on December 2, 2002.[39] The purpose of these amendments is to clarify the application of standard, assessment, and accountability provisions to pupils "with the most significant cognitive disabilities." Under the regulations, states and LEAs may adopt alternative assessments *based on alternative achievement standards* — aligned with the state's academic content standards and reflecting "professional judgment of the highest achievement standards possible" — for a limited percentage of pupils with disabilities.[40] When making AYP determinations, in general no more than 1.0% of all pupils (approximately 9% of all pupils with disabilities) counted as having achievement levels of proficient or above may consist of pupils taking such alternative assessments based on alternative achievement standards at the state and LEA level; there is no such limitation for individual schools. SEAs may request from the U.S. Secretary of Education an exception allowing them to exceed the 1.0% cap statewide, and SEAs may grant such exceptions to LEAs within their state.

In addition, ED published supplementary "non-regulatory draft guidance" on these standard and assessment requirements, as well as those related to NAEP participation, on March 10, 2003.[41] This document is intended to provide guidance which is consistent with that in the regulations discussed above, but is more detailed. This guidance specifically provides that states must include in their ESEA consolidated application/plan academic content standards in reading/language arts and mathematics for each of grades 3-8, as well as a detailed timeline for meeting subsequent deadlines for the development and implementation of assessments in these subjects and grades, plus standards and assessments at three grade levels in science, by *May 1, 2003*.

Steps Toward Implementation of the NAEP Requirements. In the period since enactment of the NCLBA, a number of steps have been taken toward implementation of the new requirements for state participation in NAEP. First, the schedule for test administration has been revised to provide for administration of state NAEP tests in 4th and 8th grade reading and mathematics every two years, beginning with the 2002-2003 school year (spring 2003). Initial NAEP 4th and 8th grade Reading and mathematics results for all states were released in November 2003. Further, as is discussed in a later section of this report, the NAGB has published a report, "Using the National Assessment of Educational Progress to Confirm State Test Results," which examines issues related to the possible use of state NAEP results to "confirm" trends in state assessment results.

At the same time, NAGB has established, and NCES has begun to implement, several changes to NAEP policies and practices that are supportive of, or were adopted primarily in response to, the expanded role for NAEP under the NCLBA.[42] In recognition of the increased emphasis on measurement of performance gaps among different demographic groups of pupils in the NCLBA, more questions are being added at the upper and lower ends of the difficulty range, so that achievement gaps among pupil groups can be more reliably measured. In addition, studies are being conducted of possible ways to adjust sampling strategy in order to assure adequate numbers of pupils in the various demographic groups referenced in the NCLBA.

At the same time, a number of administrative adjustments are being implemented that are intended to reduce required pupil sample sizes in the aggregate (e.g., the main NAEP state and national pupil samples will be combined for the first time), although samples of pupils will likely be increased in small and/or sparsely populated states in order to enhance the precision of results. Efforts are being made to minimize time demands, with a goal of reporting results of reading and mathematics assessments within six months of test administration.

Special issues arise with respect to Puerto Rico, which is treated as a state under ESEA Title I-A, but has not previously participated in state NAEP tests. A basic problem is that selected NAEP mathematics tests have been translated into and administered (to LEP pupils) in Spanish, but there are no Spanish versions of the NAEP reading tests. Aside from the task of translation, questions arise about the comparability of tests administered in different languages, especially in subjects such as reading. Currently, NAGB plans to administer NAEP mathematics tests to 4th and 8th grade pupils in Puerto Rico beginning in 2003, but policy will not be established regarding development and administration of NAEP reading tests there until a future date.

Finally, state NAEP tests will now be administered by contractors, rather than (as in the past) local teachers; there will be a full-time NAEP coordinator in every state, and a State Service Center will be established to support these coordinators; and NAGB has established procedures for limited public access to NAEP test items, and for submission, review, and resolution of complaints about NAEP tests by parents and other members of the public.

Issues Regarding the Expanded ESEA Title I-APupil Assessment Requirements

What Types of Assessments Would Meet the Expanded Assessment Requirements?

As described above, the NCLBA includes explicit reference to a number of criteria which state assessments must meet in order to comply with the ESEA Title I-A requirements. However, the statute does not appear to directly or explicitly address two major issues with respect to the assessments: (a) whether qualifying state assessment systems must include only CRTs, or they may include a mix of CRTs and NRTs, as long as the latter are modified to provide the required linkage to state content and achievement standards; and (b) whether qualifying state assessment systems must include only assessments which are the same statewide (except in states which lack authority to require statewide assessments), or whether they may include a mixture of statewide and locally varying assessments, as long as the latter are deemed to be "equivalent" and adequately linked to state content and achievement standards. It is stated that assessments must "be the same academic assessments used to measure the achievement of all children" (Section 1111(b)(3)(C)(i)), but the implications of this provision are ambiguous in cases where a state has no assessment to measure the achievement of all children in certain grades.

Arguably, criterion-referenced assessments which are administered to all public school pupils statewide in the relevant grades are most fully consistent with the requirements which are explicitly stated in Title I-A. Only CRTs are designed comprehensively and "from the ground up" to measure pupil achievement with respect to specific content and academic achievement standards. While certain NRTs may be somewhat related to state standards in their generic form, with substantial overlap in test items with CRTs, and more closely related if modified specifically for this purpose, as would be required under the regulations, they are nevertheless initially designed primarily for the purpose of ranking and sorting pupils, not for the purpose of determining whether pupils meet state-determined achievement levels. In fact, it is not yet clear whether modified versions of assessments designed *initially* as NRTs can indeed meet the Title I-A requirements for linkage with state content and performance standards; some states, such as California, have attempted to meet the 1994 assessment requirements through use of modified NRTs, but no such assessments have yet been fully approved by ED.[43]

Similarly, assessments that are the same statewide would seem to most fully meet the purposes of Title I-A, especially with respect to the use of assessment results to determine whether schools or LEAs meet state standards of adequate yearly progress (AYP). The best way to assure that assessments of the extent to which pupils meet state achievement standards are equivalent and consistent statewide is to use the same assessments throughout the state. This is especially important in view of the use of assessment results to determine whether schools or LEAs meet AYP standards, and the need to aggregate local results to determine whether states overall meet such requirements. Establishing equivalence among varying local tests might be possible, but is likely to be very difficult. According to a recent National Research Council report, "Under limited conditions it may be possible to calculate a linkage between two tests, but multiple factors affect the validity of inferences that may be drawn from the linked scores. These factors include the context, format, and margin of error of the tests; the intended and actual uses of the tests; and the consequences attached to the results of the tests."[44] Further, there is no precedent for allowing states to meet Title I-A assessment requirements through use of different assessments in different LEAs — except for the two states which may lack authority to establish statewide assessments, no states have been allowed to meet the 1994 standard and assessment requirements through use of locally-varying assessments.

Articulation between the tests used in different grades, and coherence of the overall assessment system, are also important concerns. If, for example, statewide tests are used in some grades but locally varying tests in other grades, or if CRTs are used in some grades and modified NRTs in others, this would likely create significant articulation difficulties, with variations from grade to grade in the proportion of pupils meeting state standards which result solely from the assessment instrument used, separate from any underlying differences in achievement levels.

Criteria established in the regulations published by ED for mixed state assessment systems are relatively demanding. Any NRTs used must be augmented to "measure accurately the depth and breadth of the State's academic content standards" (34 CFR 200.3(a)(2)(ii)(A)), and have results expressed in terms of the state's achievement standards;

and any LEA-selected assessments used to meet the Title I-A requirements must be of "equivalent to one another ... in their content coverage, difficulty and quality," have "comparable validity and reliability," and produce results which can be aggregated (34 CFR 200.3(c)(2)). If these criteria were to be strictly interpreted by ED in the assessment review process, it is likely to be very difficult for mixed state assessment systems to be approved. However, opponents of proposals to allow states to meet the Title I-A requirements through mixed assessment systems are concerned that ED's review process may not be very strict, and that in some states, systems may be approved which are not well aligned with state standards or are not consistent among LEAs statewide, at least in certain grades, with the result that the standards for determining whether schools are meeting AYP standards would significantly vary among LEAs.

In contrast, proponents of a relatively high degree of state flexibility in meeting the Title I-A requirements through mixed assessment systems argue that this will minimize federal influence and intrusion, recognize state primacy in selecting assessment systems which meet their needs, minimize costs, and still meet the purposes of Title I-A because of the criteria which such systems would have to meet. Proponents of allowing the use of modified NRTs to meet the requirements, at least for some grades, argue that the differences between NRTs and CRTs have more to do with how test results are analyzed and presented than with the test items themselves. The fact that several states currently use a mix of statewide CRTs in some grades and NRTs in others, or statewide tests of either type in some grades and locally varying tests in others, may indicate that such mixed assessment systems meet important educational needs and goals, as perceived by the states themselves.

How Strict Will Be ED's Review of State Assessment Systems, and Will States Meet Requirements on Schedule?

While distinct, this issue is related to the topic discussed immediately above, since the likelihood that states will meet statutory deadlines will in many cases be significantly influenced by the degree of flexibility to include a variety of tests (NRTs and CRTs, locally varying and statewide tests) in state assessment systems. The greater the allowed degree of flexibility, the easier it will be for states to modify existing assessment systems to meet the expanded Title I-A requirements. However, the rigor of ED's review of state assessment systems is a somewhat more independent factor — a high or low degree of strictness may accompany either a broad or narrow range of flexibility in the requirements being enforced.

As indicated by the relevant policy guidance and the published communications to states, peer reviewers and ED staff appear to have been conducting relatively rigorous and detailed reviews of the "evidence" submitted by states regarding whether their assessment systems meet the "1994 requirements" initiated by the IASA. The features which the Title I-A statute requires state assessment systems to exhibit are themselves numerous and relatively detailed, and a substantial implementation of them is likely to involve somewhat exhaustive review. The assessment reviews have focused especially on issues regarding testing, score reporting, and inclusion in accountability systems for LEP pupils and those with disabilities. While there are complex issues and considerations in these areas, they are not being raised solely, and possibly not even primarily, because of the Title I-A requirements. For example, while there are general guidelines, applicable under Title VI of the Civil Rights Act of 1964 to any LEA receiving federal grants, regarding the use of an appropriate language and/or other accommodations for assessment of LEP pupils,[45] and requirements under the IDEA for alternate assessments where necessary for pupils with disabilities, it is largely in the context of Title I-A that such requirements are having an impact because of the scrutiny currently being given to whether state assessments meet the Title I-A requirements.

While it may be questioned whether ED should be reviewing state assessment systems in such detail, this scrutiny may be necessary to enforce Title I-A's statutory requirements, and might also be necessary to establish outcome accountability for all major groups of disadvantaged pupils. If, for example, significant numbers of LEP pupils or those with disabilities were excluded from state assessments, or were not provided with appropriate accommodations, then it would be impossible to determine whether they, along with the pupil population in general, are adequately meeting state performance goals. Such inclusive assessment, combined with disaggregated score reporting, becomes increasingly important as focus shifts toward outcome measures to assure accountability for use of federal aid funds, and Title I-A programs are increasingly conducted in a school wide program format, in which services are not targeted on the individual pupils with lowest achievement in a participating school.[46]

While detailed review by ED of state assessment systems may raise concerns about undue federal influence over this fundamental aspect of state and local public education systems, there are many statutory limitations on the review process. As noted earlier, the federal government is prohibited from mandating, directing, or controlling a state's, LEA's, or school's standards, assessments, or curriculum; states may not be required to submit their standards to ED; and no state plan may be disapproved by ED on the basis of specific content or achievement standards or assessment items or instruments. Nevertheless, the degree of federal influence over at least the broad parameters of state pupil assessment systems — such as grades and subject areas tested, inclusion of special needs pupil groups, disaggregated reporting of results — will increase as the NCLBA provisions are fully implemented.

A recent paper by a former ED official who was largely responsible for the initial stages of review of state compliance with the "1994 requirements" under ESEA Title I-A encourages continuation of a "vigorous" approach by ED to enforcement of these requirements — "being prepared to use a full range of enforcement strategies — from jawboning to compliance agreements to withholding administrative or program funds if necessary" even though ED has not had "a strong record of compliance monitoring in ESEA programs."[47] In contrast, others have urged ED staff to emphasize flexibility in reviewing state compliance with assessment and related requirements under the NCLBA — "We would advise those involved in the rulemaking and guidance process to proceed cautiously, for the very vagueness of the law ... is actually an asset, as it leaves each state room to experiment within its own strengths and limitations."[48] It is not yet clear whether, or how, the nature and rigor of this review process may change with more complete implementation of the NCLBA.

The rigor of ED's assessment review process, and the flexibility of the assessment regulations, will also likely influence the extent to which states meet the expanded requirements on schedule. A recent General Accounting Office report identified four additional factors which have influenced the pace of state compliance with Title I-A assessment requirements: "(1) the efforts of state leaders to make Title I compliance a priority; (2) coordination between staff of different agencies and levels of government; (3) obtaining buy-in from local administrators, educators, and parents; and (4) the availability of state level expertise."[49]

Given the experience thus far with the "1994 requirements," as described above, it seems likely that a significant number of states may fail to meet the future assessment deadlines in the NCLBA. ED is prohibited from granting additional waivers, or negotiating additional compliance agreements, with respect to the *1994* requirements, and the NCLBA requires ED to apply sanctions to states which fail to meet their modified deadlines for those requirements. However, there are no similar limits on the possible granting of waivers (under the general ESEA waiver authority in Title IX, Part D), and no *required* sanctions (although the sanction of reducing state administration grants is authorized), for states which fail to meet the *new* assessment requirement deadlines in the NCLBA.

What Will Be the Cost of Developing and Implementing the Required Assessments, and to What Extent Will Federal Grants Be Available to Pay for Them?

The addition of requirements to conduct annual assessments in at least four more grades than required previously, and to include standards and assessments at three grade levels in science, will require most states to significantly increase their expenditures for standard and test development and administration. As indicated earlier, it is very difficult, if not impossible, to specify all of these potential costs with precision. Existing estimates of actual state and/or local expenditures for assessment programs are incomplete, and they refer only to direct, state-level costs for current testing programs, not to the expanded assessments required under the NCLBA.

The NCLBA conference report directs the General Accounting Office to conduct a study of the costs to each state of developing and administering the assessments required under Title I-A, both overall and for each of fiscal years 2002-2008; however, no information is yet available from that study. At least two organizations have attempted during 2001-2002 to estimate costs for states of meeting assessment requirements similar to those of the NCLBA. In 2001, the National Association of State Boards of Education (NASBE) estimated that the new grade 3-8 assessments (only) would cost states between \$2.7 and \$7.0 billion in the aggregate over a seven-year period.[50] On an annual basis, *if* costs were equally distributed across the seven years, this would represent a range of \$386 million to \$1 billion per year. In contrast, Accountability Works, a private consulting firm, recently estimated that the annual cost of meeting all of the new assessment requirements in the NCLBA would be approximately \$312 million for each of 2002-2003 and 2003-2004, \$388 million for each of 2004-2005 and 2005-2006, and \$328 million for each of 2006-2007 and 2007-2008.[51]

Each of these estimates is based on a number of assumptions which may or may not prove to be valid in practice, and the NASBE study was based on portions of the original Bush Administration proposal, not the final version of the NCLBA. For example, the NASBE study considers only the requirement for annual standards-based assessments in mathematics and reading in each of grades 3-8, not the science assessment requirement; is based on the original proposal that grade 3-8 assessments must be implemented in 2004-2005, rather than 2005-2006; does not seem to incorporate an assumption that development costs will decline at any point of the life cycle of assessments; and incorporates an assumption that test development costs will rise continuously with the number of pupils in a state, with no adjustment for economies of scale. The Accountability Works study assumes that all states already meet the assessment requirements under the 1994 IASA (whereas only 21 do so currently); incorporates assumed levels of annual test development and administration costs which appear to be based on data from only two states; excludes costs for SEA staff and overhead; and incorporates an assumed amount for annual test administration costs ($10 per pupil) which would not be consistent with use of essay or other extended response (and relatively expensive to score) questions. Further, *neither* of these studies accounts for variation among the states in the extent to which they already administer standards-based assessments in reading and mathematics in each of grades 3-8 plus science assessments at three grade levels; and the basis for some of the assumptions in each of the studies is unclear.

The NCLBA authorizes $400 million for FY2002, and "such sums as may be necessary" for a number of subsequent years, for state assessment development and administration grants. The administration, although not the development, of the grade 3-8 assessments may be delayed by 1 year for each year that the minimum amounts (e.g., $390 million for FY2004) are *not* appropriated (the minimum amount has been appropriated for each of FY2002-2004). The available information on *current* levels of direct, state-level expenditures for testing programs indicate that the "trigger" appropriation levels for state assessment grants are, in the aggregate, somewhat lower than these estimates.[52] The "trigger" amounts are also somewhat above the Accountability Works estimate of *future* costs, approximately the same as the minimum NASBE estimate, and well below the upper NASBE estimate.

It is clear that the costs of meeting the expanded assessment requirements will vary widely from state to state, not only because of differences in state size, but also particularly because of substantial differences in the extent to which state-mandated tests in reading and mathematics are already administered to all pupils in grades 3-8, or tests in science are administered to pupils in selected grade ranges, and whether the existing tests meet the Title I-A technical requirements of alignment with state standards, inclusion of all pupil groups, etc. As of the 2001-2002 school year, 15 states administered tests in reading and mathematics in each of grades 3-8, and 24 states administered tests in at least three grade levels in science, but it is unclear how many of these tests are adequately aligned with state content and achievement standards.[53]

With respect to the distribution among the states of funds for test development and administration, the NCLBA provides for allocation of a substantial share (43% for FY2002) of these funds in equal amounts to each state, with the remainder allocated in proportion to children and youth aged 5-17 years. The allocation formula does not recognize the substantial variation in the extent to which states currently administer the required assessments, and therefore face varying increases in assessment program costs. The allocation of funds by formula to all states, regardless of the current status of their state assessment policies and programs, might recognize that all states face ongoing costs, and might possibly reward states which have already adopted relatively extensive assessment programs. At the same time, the formula does not target funds on the states with the greatest needs.

What Might Be the Impact of the Requirement for Annual Assessment of English Language Proficiency of LEP Pupils?

As noted earlier, the NCLBA requires states to provide that their LEAs will annually assess the English language proficiency of their LEP pupils, beginning in the 2002-2003 school year. This is separate from the requirements regarding treatment of LEP pupils in states' general assessment systems — i.e., the requirement that LEP pupils be included in such assessments, in which they are to be assessed in a valid and reliable manner and provided with "reasonable" accommodations, in the language and form most likely to yield accurate and reliable information on what they know and can do in academic content areas (in subjects other than English itself), with pupils who have attended schools in the United States (excluding Puerto Rico) for 3 or more consecutive school years to be assessed in English.

In contrast to such requirements regarding treatment of LEP pupils in states' general assessment systems, the separate requirement for annual assessments of English language proficiency lacks specificity. There are no statutory details regarding technical characteristics of the tests — except that the assessment must consider the pupils' oral, reading, and writing skills — and (thus far) no policy guidance from ED. It is also somewhat ambiguous regarding whether states or LEAs are ultimately or primarily responsible for implementing this requirement.

Depending on possible future regulations or policy guidance from ED, this new requirement may lead to relatively little change in current activities in LEAs. Although comprehensive and detailed surveys of such assessment practices are not currently available, there is substantial evidence that LEAs in general already assess the English language proficiency of LEP pupils for purposes of placement in instructional programs, determination of needed accommodations in general assessment programs, evaluation of programs targeted on LEP pupils, and movement of pupils from special programs to mainstream instruction. While a variety of assessment methods are used, including teacher observation and home language surveys, recent surveys indicate that a large majority of LEAs administer formal English language proficiency tests to their LEP (or potentially LEP) pupils.[54] Policy guidance from ED's Office for Civil Rights indicates that such assessments should be undertaken especially, but not only, for purposes of assigning pupils to instructional programs targeted at LEP pupils, determining the timing of transition to regular or mainstream instruction for such pupils, and evaluating the effectiveness of special programs for LEP pupils; although this guidance is unspecific regarding the type of assessment LEAs should use.[55]

In addition, LEAs participating in the new English Language Acquisition program authorized under ESEA Title III, Part A, must report annually the number and percentage of participating pupils who attain English proficiency, as determined by a "valid and reliable assessment of English proficiency" (Section 3121(a)(3)). If ED's future policy guidance is consistent with the statute's lack of specificity regarding the new Title I-A requirement, there may be little required change in LEA activities as a result of the requirement.

What Might Be the Impact of Requiring State Participation in NAEP?

Possible Influence on State Standards and Assessments Arising from (Marginally) Increased Stakes. Two key characteristics of the NAEP program since its inception have been: (1) the content frameworks, upon which test items are based, have been independent of the content standards adopted by any state or national organization; and (2) the "stakes" associated with performance on the tests have been extremely low. The NCLBA's requirement for states to participate in NAEP in order to retain eligibility for ESEA Title I-A grants, with the implicit purpose of using the results to "confirm" performance trends on state-selected assessments, has potential implications for both of these characteristics of NAEP.

Previously, the only "stakes" associated with state participation in NAEP have been the symbolic ones arising from public dissemination of NAEP results for states that chose to participate and which allowed their assessment results to be published. Public attention to these results, among persons other than selected policymakers, researchers, and policy analysts, seems to have been limited. The NAEP scores have had no impact on state finances or eligibility for federal programs or services.

While state involvement with NAEP will change significantly under the NCLBA, the stakes for states will remain relatively low. State results will be published as an implicit "confirmation" of test score trends on state assessments, but these NAEP scores will still have no direct impact on state eligibility for federal assistance. Provisions of the House- and Senate-passed versions of the NCLBA for state bonuses and sanctions based in part on NAEP score trends were eliminated from the conference version. Under the NCLBA as enacted, ED is required to establish a peer review process to evaluate whether states have met their statewide AYP goals; states which fail to meet them are to be listed in an annual report to Congress, and technical assistance is to be provided to states that fail to meet their goals for 2 consecutive years. State NAEP scores will likely be considered in this review process. However, there is no provision for state bonuses or sanctions under this procedure, only publicity and technical assistance. This increases the "stakes" associated with state NAEP performance, but only to a very modest degree.

Nevertheless, even a small increase in the stakes associated with state performance on NAEP tests attracts attention to the possibility that NAEP frameworks and test items might influence state standards and assessments. To the extent that the required participation in NAEP increases attention to state performance on these tests, there might be a basis for concern that states would have an incentive to modify their curriculum content standards to more closely resemble the NAEP test frameworks. To counteract this potential problem, the NCLBA prohibits the use of NAEP assessments by agents of the federal government to influence state or LEA instructional programs or assessments. However, subtle, indirect, and/or unintended forms of influence may be impossible to detect or prohibit. A "White Paper" policy statement released by NAGB on May 18, 2002, attempts to distinguish between "active attempts ... to persuade others to adopt NAEP policies, procedures, or content," which are prohibited, and "influence by good example," which (according to this document) is not.

Voluntary Participation by LEAs, Schools, and Pupils. Might a conflict arise between the requirement for NAEP participation by states participating in ESEA Title I-A and the provision that participation in NAEP tests is voluntary for all pupils, schools, and possibly LEAs? While participation by states, LEAs, schools, and pupils was voluntary under previous *federal* law and policy, states or LEAs were not prohibited from requiring participation by LEAs, schools, or pupils under their own laws or policies. However, as noted earlier (p. 13), there are conflicting statutory and regulatory provisions regarding participation in NAEP tests by LEAs and schools which may be selected for NAEP test administration.

Some have expressed concern that the new provisions regarding voluntary participation in NAEP might lead to two types of difficulties: (a) in a time of likely increased assessment activity for pupils nationwide, resistance to participation in NAEP might grow to an extent that it threatens the quality of the national sample of tested pupils and makes it difficult to maintain trend lines; and (b) more specifically, states might be stuck between a requirement to participate in NAEP and an inability to recruit a sufficiently large sample of LEAs, schools, and pupils to participate in order to produce valid and reliable assessment results. In the recent past, some states have attempted to participate in NAEP but found themselves unable to induce sufficient numbers of LEAs or schools to do so.[56]

The primary counter to this concern is that the policies regarding voluntary participation in NAEP have changed only modestly. As far as federal policies are concerned, participation has already been voluntary at all levels. While states or LEAs previously could have mandated participation by LEAs, schools, or pupils, apparently they generally attempted to avoid doing so. Thus, in practice, little may have changed. There may nevertheless be some cause for concern, with the expansion of NAEP to states which have not previously chosen to participate.

Can NAEP Results Be Used to "Confirm" State Test Score Trends? An unstated, but clearly implicit, purpose of the state NAEP participation requirement is to "confirm" trends in pupil achievement, as measured by state-selected assessments by comparing them with trends in NAEP results. Some have questioned whether it is possible or appropriate to use results on one assessment to "confirm" results on another assessment which may have been developed very differently, and what form this "confirmation" might take.

State assessments vary widely in terms of several important characteristics — such as the content and skills which they are designed to assess, their format, and modes of response — and they are likely to continue to vary widely, especially as the final assessment regulations allow the use of both CRTs and modified NRTs, as well as locally varying assessments. As a result, some state assessments will be much more similar to NAEP in these important respects than others, and there will be consequent variation in the significance of similarities or differences when comparing trends in NAEP versus state assessment score trends for pupils.

If, for example, a state test is closely aligned to state curriculum content standards which are substantially different from the content embodied in NAEP assessment frameworks, and if instruction is modified to better match the state standards, then it is possible that scores on the state assessment will rise while those on NAEP will be flat or even decline. NAEP frameworks are designed with the intention that they substantially reflect state standards *on average*; according to a recent analysis, "States vary in the amount that their assessment domains [i.e., the content and skills covered by the assessments] overlap with NAEP. For some, there is almost complete overlap. For others, the overlap is modest."[57] Other major differences between NAEP and state assessments include: (a) the time of year when tests are administered; (b) relative placement of cut scores for achievement levels; (c) the (often high, but varying) stakes associated with state assessments versus the low stakes associated with NAEP; and (d) test format and modes of response.

As for the form which a comparison of NAEP and state test scores might take, two obvious candidates are average raw scores and the percentages of pupils at different achievement levels (basic, proficient, etc.). While these are key benchmarks, either alone, or even both, might overlook important changes or differences in the distribution of pupil scores. For example, the scores of several pupils might improve but not by enough to raise them above the cut score for the next highest achievement level. As noted above, the NAGB has published a report, "Using the National Assessment of Educational Progress to Confirm State Test Results," whose authors argue that state NAEP scores can be used as evidence to confirm the general trends in scores on individual state assessments, although such confirmation should not be viewed as, or take the form of, a strict statistical "validation" of state test results. They address the question of whether comparisons should be based on raw scores or percentages of pupils at various achievement levels by recommending a new method of comparison which considers changes and differences in the overall achievement score distribution, not focusing solely on overall averages or cut scores.[58]

What Are the Likely Benefits and Costs of the Expanded Title I-A Assessment Requirements?

This report concludes with a review of major potential benefits and costs of the expanded pupil assessment requirements of ESEA Title I-A. The primary benefit from annual administration of a consistent series of standards-based tests would be the provision of timely information on the performance of pupils, schools, and LEAs, throughout most of the elementary and middle school grades. While a majority of pupils have already been taking assessments in many of grades 3-8, these have been typically a mix of CRTs and NRTs, state-mandated and locally selected tests, with no provision that most of these are either equivalent statewide or aligned to state content and achievement standards. Even under the broadest interpretation of ED's draft policy guidance, which would allow states to use modified NRTs in addition to CRTs, and locally varying tests which are deemed to be equivalent, the resulting state assessment systems would be more coherent, consistent, and well-articulated than the current systems in most states. The availability of such consistent, annual assessment results would be of value for both diagnostic and accountability purposes. The resulting assessment systems would also continuously emphasize the importance of meeting state standards as embodied by the assessments.

These expanded requirements regarding pupil assessments — and school, LEA, and state accountability based on performance on the assessments — have been enacted in the context of a broader strategy, also initiated in the 1994 ESEA amendments and expanded by the NCLBA, which involves increased state and local flexibility in the use of federal education assistance funds.[59] Under this strategy, accountability for appropriate use of federal aid funds is to be established more on the basis of pupil performance outcomes, and less on prescribed procedures or targeting of resources, than in the past. Such a strategy implicitly relies heavily on high quality, current, detailed, and widely disseminated information on pupil achievement as a basis for outcome accountability policies and procedures. It is desirable that achievement data be as comparable and current as possible while not compromising the primacy of states and LEAs in setting K-12 education policy.

According to a recent ED publication, "Testing for Results, Helping Families, Schools and Communities Understand and Improve Student Achievement,"[60] annual standards-based assessments "will empower parents, citizens, educators, administrators and policymakers with data ... in annual report cards on school performance and on statewide progress." Further, "The tests will give teachers and principals information about how each child is performing and help them to diagnose and meet the needs of each student. They will also give policymakers and leaders at the state and local levels critical information about which schools and school districts are succeeding and why, so this success may be expanded and any failures addressed.... A good evaluation system provides invaluable information that can inform instruction and curriculum, help diagnose achievement problems and inform decision making in the classroom, the school, the district and the home. Testing is about providing useful information and it can change the way schools operate."

At the same time, the expanded Title I-A assessment requirements might lead to a variety of costs, or unintended consequences, in both financial and other forms. One such "cost" is expanded federal influence on state and local education policies. Assuming that most, if not all, states will choose to implement them in order to maintain Title I-A eligibility,[61] then assessment requirements attached to an aid program focused on *disadvantaged pupils* would broadly influence policies regarding standards, assessments, and accountability affecting *all pupils* in the participating states. This would represent a substantial increase in federal influence in the assessment and accountability aspects of K-12 education policy.

In the majority of states which have not administered a consistent series of mandated, standards-based assessments in each of grades 3-8, this policy may have resulted primarily from cost or time constraints, or the states may have determined that annual testing of this sort is not educationally appropriate, or at least that its benefits are not equal to the relevant costs. These costs may include not only the direct costs of test development, administration, scoring, reporting, etc., not all of which may be paid through federal assessment grants, but also an increased risk of "over-emphasis" on preparation for the tests, especially if the tests do not adequately assess the full range of knowledge and skills which schools are expected to impart.

The authors of a recent study of the effects of high stakes assessment policies in 18 states have posited an "Uncertainty Principle," which may be relevant to such concerns — "The more important that any quantitative social indicator becomes in social decision-making, the more likely it will be to distort and corrupt the social process it is intended to monitor."[62] At the least, annual testing of pupils in grades 3-8 would increase the importance of having tests which are well-designed and closely linked to state content and achievement standards which are truly challenging.

Nevertheless, even within the specific realm of standards and assessments, federal influence is and would remain limited in several important respects. With the exception of the limited role of state NAEP tests, the standards and assessments would be totally selected by the states. ED would not have any authority to review the substance of any state standards, and no state plan may be disapproved by ED on the basis of specific content or achievement standards or test items or instruments.

Ultimately, whether increased federal influence in certain respects, combined with less federal control over certain other aspects of state and local use of federal aid funds, is a "balanced tradeoff" is a subjective political judgment. The key analytical point is that the proposed increase in federal influence is constrained, and is balanced by a decrease of federal influence in certain other respects.

References

[1] Much of the data in this section is derived from: *No State Left Behind: The Challenges and Opportunities of ESEA 2001*, by the Education Commission of the States, available at [http://www.ecs.org]; and *Assessment and Accountability Systems: 50 State Profiles*, by the Consortium for Policy Research in Education, available at [http://www.cpre.org/ Publications/Publications_Accountability.htm].

[2] While Iowa does not mandate participation in any specific assessment, tests developed by the Iowa Testing Programs at the University of Iowa and published nationwide by Riverside Publishing are administered to a large majority of pupils attending public K-12 schools in Iowa, on the basis of voluntary decisions by each LEA.

[3] Three of the largest such commercial test publishers are: (1) CTB/McGraw-Hill, at [http://www.ctb.com/]; Riverside (Houghton Mifflin) Publishing, at [http://www.riverpub.com/products/groupindex.html]; and Harcourt Assessment, at [https://marketplace.psychcorp.com/PsychCorp/International.aspx].

[4] An example of such a consortium is the New Standards Project, a joint effort of several states and LEAs, the National Center on Education and The Economy, and the Learning Research and Development Center at the University of Pittsburgh.

[5] analyzed, but also typically differ to some degree with respect to such characteristics as the range of questions included.

[6] For example, in order to clarify distinctions between high- and low-achieving pupils, a norm-referenced test will typically include some very difficult questions that only a few pupils can answer, and some very easy questions that almost all pupils can answer correctly. Test content and questions are selected largely on the basis of how efficiently they rank pupils. In contrast, a CRT would be focused solely on the relevant content standards, with no direct emphasis on distinguishing the highest- from the lowest-achieving pupils.

[7] Direct expenditures include those for such activities and services as development and field testing of assessments, purchase of test materials, scoring, or dissemination of results. Indirect expenditures might include those for time spent by teachers and other staff preparing pupils for or administering assessments or overhead costs. For a review of related issues, see Richard P. Phelps, *Estimating the Costs of Standardized Student Testing in the United States*, Journal of Education Finance, winter 2000, pp. 343-380.

[8] Available on the Internet at [http://www.stateline.org].

[9] See Education Commission of the States, *Estimated Per-Student Spending on Statewide Testing Programs*, Oct. 2001. Available at [http://www.ecs.org].

[10] Lawrence O. Picus, *Estimating the Costs of Student Assessment in North Carolina and Kentucky: A State-Level Analysis*, CRESST Technical Report 408, Feb. 1996.

[11] See CRS Report RS21094, *Adequate Yearly Progress Under ESEA Title I: Estimates for Three States Based on Specifications in H.R. 1 Conference Agreement*, by David P. Smole and Wayne C. Riddle.

[12] As is discussed later in this report, most states did not meet this deadline, established in the 1994 IASA.

[13] There is explicit authority for a one-year delay of this requirement in cases of exceptional or uncontrollable circumstances.

[14] There is some obvious overlap in these requirements — e.g., states meeting the requirement for assessments in reading and math at three grade levels already meet the requirements for 1 or 2 of grades 3-8.

[15] Separately, the provisions regarding AYP provide that at least 95% of the pupils in each demographic group within each school must be included in the assessments in order for the school to meet AYP requirements. Pupils may be excluded from school-level score reporting and accountability if they have attended a specific school for less than one year.

[16] LEAs may continue to administer assessments to pupils in non-English languages for up to five years if, on a case-by-case basis, they determine that this would likely yield more accurate information on what the students know and can do.

[17] A one-year waiver of this requirement is specifically authorized in cases of exceptional or uncontrollable circumstances.

[18] Similar, although somewhat less specific, language may be found in ESEA Section9526(b)(1) and Section 9527(a).

[19] For additional information on NAEP, see CRS Report 98-348, National Assessment of Educational Progress: Background and Reauthorization Issues, by Wayne Riddle.

[20] Additional long-term trend assessments in writing and science were last administered in1999. There is no current plan to administer the writing assessment in the future; revised science assessment test items are being developed, and may be administered in the future.

[21] An NAGB policy adopted in May 2002 addresses this concern with respect to the science assessment, and some changes will be made to the content of the science assessment before its next administration.

[22] The Voluntary National Test proposal of the Clinton Administration was to develop individual versions of the NAEP 4th grade reading and 8th grade math tests (see CRS Report97-774, National Tests: Administration Initiative, by Wayne Riddle). Activity related to this proposal has been terminated.

[23] Once states decided to participate they were not prohibited from mandating participation by LEAs or schools under state and local law, although it appears that most states have always attempted to obtain LEA and school participation through voluntary recruitment.

[24] For a description of the Trial Urban Assessment, and available results, see[http://nces.ed.gov/nationsreportcard/reading/results2002/districtresults.asp].

[25] The role of NAEP in "confirming" state test score trends is not explicitly stated in the final statute, but is explicitly mentioned in ED documents, such as the following: "Confirming Progress — Under H.R. 1 a small sample of students in each state will participate in the 4th and 8th grade National Assessment of Educational Progress (NAEP) in reading and math every other year in order to help the U.S. Department of Education verify the results of statewide assessments required under Title I to demonstrate student performance and progress." See *Using the National Assessment of Educational Progress to Confirm State Test Results*, prepared by an Ad Hoc Committee on Confirming Test Results, National Assessment Governing Board, at [http://www.nagb.org].

[26] See CRS Report RL31353, *Educational Research, Statistics, and Evaluation: Legislation in the 107th Congress*, by Paul M. Irwin.

[27] Peer reviewers have relied primarily upon the Department's *Peer Reviewer Guidance for Evaluating Evidence of Final Assessments Under Title I of the Elementary and Secondary Education Act* (available at [http://www.ed.gov/policy/elsec/guid/cpg.pdf]) to guide their activities. While this document was published before enactment of the NCLBA, it remains applicable, at least for the present, mainly because most applicable underlying requirements are essentially unchanged.

[28] The pre-NCLBA version also specifically authorized the Secretary of Education to waive the deadline for assessment implementation for an additional year if necessary to correct problems that were identified in field testing; the current ESEA authorizes specific waivers for up to 1 year for full implementation of the new requirements for annual assessments in grades 3-8, and assessment of the English language proficiency of LEP pupils, in cases of "exceptional and unforeseen circumstances," and authorizes states to delay implementation of the grade 3-8 requirement if minimum amounts are not appropriated for state assessment grants.

[29] The compliance agreements for 4 of the 5 states have been published in the *Federal Register* on Feb. 20 (Alabama and Idaho), Feb. 21 (West Virginia), and Mar. 24 (Montana), 2003.

[30] U.S. Department of Education press release dated Apr. 8, 2002.

[31] These are available at [http://www.ed.gov/offices/OESE/saa/state_chart.html].

[32] Pupils who have attended schools in a LEA for one year or more, but who have attended a particular school for less than one year, may be excluded from accountability determinations for the school (but not for the LEA overall).

[33] Section 612 (a)(17) of the Individuals with Disabilities Education Act (IDEA) requires states to develop guidelines for the administration of alternate assessments for pupils with disabilities who cannot participate in state- and LEA-wide assessment programs.

[34] *Federal Register*, July 5, 2002, pp. 45038-45047. As is discussed below, proposed amendments to these regulations were published in the *Federal Register* on Mar. 20, 2003.

[35] ED's implementation of the negotiated rulemaking requirement was challenged in federal court. Four organizations (The Center on Law and Education, National Coalition for the Homeless, National Law Center on Homelessness, and Designs for Change) and an individual parent charged that parents and students were inadequately represented in the process, particularly in view of the language requiring an "equitable

balance between representatives of parents and students and representatives of educators and education officials." The negotiated rulemaking panel included 17 persons; while only 2 of the 17 persons represented parents specifically, several of the others were parents in addition to representing other groups. On May 22, 2002, the United States District Court for the District of Columbia ruled in favor of the Department of Education and the case was dismissed. An analysis of the legal issues associated with this suit is beyond the scope of this report.

[36] In the negotiated rulemaking process, which took place in mid-March 2002, the initial draft proposed regulations were changed in very few significant respects. The primary changes included: (a) it was further clarified that the assessment requirements apply only to public schools and their pupils, not to private (or home) schools; (b) for purposes of disaggregated score reporting, "pupils with disabilities" would be only those identified under the IDEA (this would exclude pupils identified only under Section 504 of the Rehabilitation Act); and (c) the criteria to be met by varying local assessments was changed from "equivalent content, rigor, and quality" and "concurrent validity" to "equivalent to one another in their content coverage, difficulty, and quality," and "comparable validity and reliability." These changes constituted essentially fine-tuning of certain points of clarification in the draft proposed regulations.

[37] In states that lack authority to require the use of the same assessments statewide (only), the assessment system may consist *entirely* of locally selected assessments.

[38] This would exclude pupils identified only under Section 504 of the Rehabilitation Act.

[39] See [http://www.ed.gov/nclb/accountability/schools/factsheet-english.html].

[40] These are discussed in CRS Report RL31487, Education for the Disadvantaged: Overview of ESEA Title I-A Amendments Under the No Child Left Behind Act, by Wayne Riddle.

[41] This limitation does *not* apply to the administration of alternative assessments *based on the same standards applicable to all students*, for other pupils with (non-cognitive or less severe cognitive) disabilities.

[42] [http://www.ed.gov/topics/topicsTier2.jsp?&top=Policy&subtop=Policy+guidance&s u btop2=Elementary+%26+secondary+education&type=T].

[43] See *NAGB Adopts Policies to Implement the No Child Left Behind Act of 2001* at [http://www.nagb.org/], plus [http://nces.ed.gov/nationsreportcard/about/current.asp].

[44] However, ED has approved the assessment systems of three other states (Delaware, Indiana, Missouri) where state-specific tests were reportedly designed from the beginning to produce both criterion-referenced and norm-referenced results. National Research Council, Uncommon Measures: Equivalence and Linkage Among Educational Tests, 1998, p. 5-4.

[45] See U.S. Department of Education, Office for Civil Rights, Testing the Academic Educational Achievement Of Limited English Proficient Students in The Use of Tests When Making High-Stakes Decisions for Students: A Resource Guide for Educators and Policymakers, a draft document dated July 6, 2000. Available on the Internet at [http://www.ed.gov/legislation/FedRegister/other/2000-4/121500b. html].

[46] There are two basic types of Title I-A programs. *Schoolwide programs* are authorized when 40% or more of the pupils in a school are from low-income families. In these

programs, Title I-A funds may be used to improve the performance of all pupils in a school, and there is no requirement to focus services on only the most disadvantaged pupils. The other major type of Title I-A service model is the *targeted assistance school* program, under which services are generally limited to the lowest achieving pupils in the school.

[47] Michael Cohen, "Implementing Title I Standards, Assessments And Accountability: Lessons From The Past, Challenges For The Future," *No Child Left Behind: What Will It Take?*, Thomas B. Fordham Foundation, Feb. 2002. pp. 84, 87.

[48] Lisa Graham Keegan, et al., "Adequate Yearly Progress: Results, not Process," *No Child Left Behind: What Will It Take?*, Thomas B. Fordham Foundation, Feb. 2002, p. 22.

[49] Title I, Education Needs to Monitor States' Scoring of Assessments, GAO-02-393, Apr. 2002, p. 13.

[50] See [http://www.nasbe.org/Archives/cost.html].

[51] See [http://www.accountabilityworks.org/publications/no_child_left_behind_test_costs pdf].

[52] The $370 million "trigger" amount (and actual appropriation) for FY2002 is 88% of the estimated aggregate expenditure level for FY2001 (discussed on p. 3 of this report) of $422.8 million.

[53] Education Commission of the States, *No State Left Behind: The Challenges and Opportunities of ESEA 2001*. Available at [http://www.ecs.org].

[54] See National Research Council, *Improving Schooling for Language-Minority Children: A Research Agenda*, 1997, pp. 115-116.

[55] See [http://www.ed.gov/about/offices/list/ocr/docs/laumemos.html].

[56] In 2000, 48 states (all except Alaska and South Dakota) initially stated their intention of participating in state NAEP, although ultimately only 41 did so. States which intended to participate, but did not do so, reportedly were unable to recruit sufficient number of LEAs and schools. See "Test Weary Schools Balk at NAEP," *Education Week*, Feb. 16, 2000.

[57] Mark D. Rekase, "Using NAEP to Confirm State Test Results: An Analysis of Issues," *Will No Child Truly Be Left Behind?*, published by the Thomas B. Fordham Foundation, Feb. 2002, p. 14.

[58] See the report for details. Available at [http://www.nagb.org].

[59] These provisions are described in CRS Report RL31284, *K-12 Education: Highlights of the No Child Left Behind Act of 2001 (P.L. 107-110)*, by Wayne Riddle. pp. 11-12.

[60] On the Internet, see [http://www.ed.gov/nclb/accountability/ayp/testingforresults.html].

[61] Officials in the state of Vermont are reportedly considering terminating their participation in Title I-A to avoid implementing expanded assessment and accountability requirements. See "Dean Urges Rejection of Federal Funds," *Burlington Free Press*, Apr. 19, 2002.

[62] Audrey L. Amrein, and David C. Berliner, *High Stakes Testing, Uncertainty, and Student Learning*. Published on the Internet at the Education Policy Analysis Archives, vol. 10, no. 18, at [http://epaa.asu.edu/epaa/v10n18/].

In: No Child Left Behind Act: Text, Interpretations and Changes ISBN 1-59454-732-7
Editor: Damian P. Olivert, pp. 61-73

Chapter 3

A GUIDE TO EDUCATION AND NO CHILD LEFT BEHIND*

U.S. Department of Education

FOREWORD

Education is one of the most important functions of government. It was a concern of the early settlers, and a focus of the Founding Fathers in writing the Constitution precisely because our democracy is dependent on an educated public. The Founders did not want education for the elite or for the many. They wanted education for all. John Adams once exclaimed: "Education for every class and rank of people down to the lowest and the poorest."

The Founding Fathers were correct: Education is necessary for the growth and prosperity of our country. As education has become more inclusive and of better quality, it has enhanced American economic and political leadership.

The task of educating the people has historically been left up to state and local governments. In the late 18th century and into the 19th century, some states, such as Virginia, Connecticut, and Pennsylvania, became known for the quality of their education systems. These school systems were the product of visionary contributions. Noah Webster worked to improve public education through writing dictionaries, spellers, readers, and histories. Benjamin Rush championed public education for girls. Horace Mann initiated efforts to improve the physical facilities of schools and to develop the first teacher training program. Thaddeus Stevens pushed through legislation I for public support of education in Pennsylvania. New York state set up the first public high schools. Other states followed, and soon public education was available for children across the country.

Recognizing the universal importance of education, the federal government assumed a larger role in financing public schools with the passage of the *Elementary and Secondary Education Act* (ESEA) in 1965. Through subsequent reauthorizations, ESEA has continued to assist the states. In 2001, the reauthorization included *No Child Left Behind,* which asks the

* From U.S. Department of Education; October, 2004.

states to set standards for student performance and teacher quality. The law establishes accountability for results and improves the inclusiveness and fairness of American education.

Sincerely,
Rod Paige
Secretary
U.S. Department of Education

EDUCATION AND THE ECONOMY

Satisfying the demand for highly skilled workers is the key to maintaining competitiveness and prosperity in the global economy.

Over the 10 years from March 1993 to March 2003, employment of persons ages 25 to 64 with master's degrees or higher increased by more than 3.2 million while employment of persons ages 25 to 64 with no more than a high school diploma increased by fewer than 460,000.[1]

Additionally, the average unemployment rate for high school dropouts in 2003 was more than 1.5 times higher than the unemployment rate for people with just high school diplomas (8.8 percent compared to 5.5 percent) and almost three times higher than the rate for college graduates (8.8 percent to 3.1 percent).[2]

A recent report found that raising student achievement directly leads to national economic growth. The report estimates that "significant improvements in education over a 20-year period could lead to as much as a 4 percent addition to the Gross Domestic Product" or over $400 billion in today's terms.[3]

EDUCATION BY THE NUMBERS

Schools and Districts

As of the 2002-03 school year, there were 14,465 public school districts in the United States.[4] The 95,615 public schools remain the primary educational delivery system in the United States.[5]

Public Schools,
by Level: 2002-03 [6]

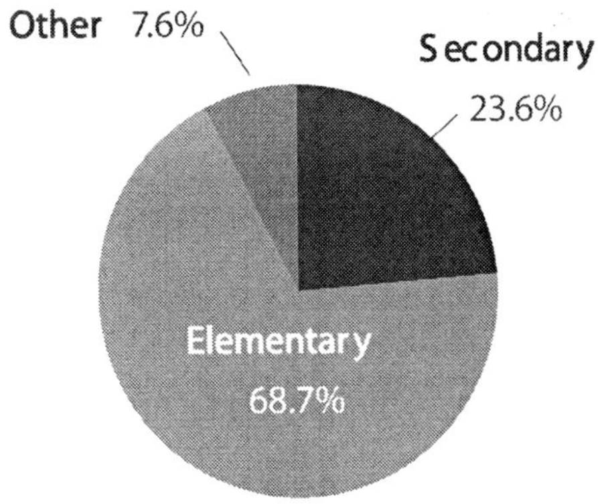

Alternative Education Systems

The number of alternative schools continues to grow as a response to the demand for more choices.

- Private Schools 27,223,223 (1999-2000)[7]
- Charer Schools 2,996 (2003-04)[8]

From 2000 to 2004 alone, more than 1,000 new charter schools opened, a 50 percent growth rate.[9]

Home Schooling

In 2004, the National Center for Education Statistics estimated that in spring 2003, the most recent period for which data is available, there were about 1.1 million home schooled children, compared to 850,000 in spring 1999. [10]

Public Elementary and Secondary
School Students, by Race: 2002-03[11]

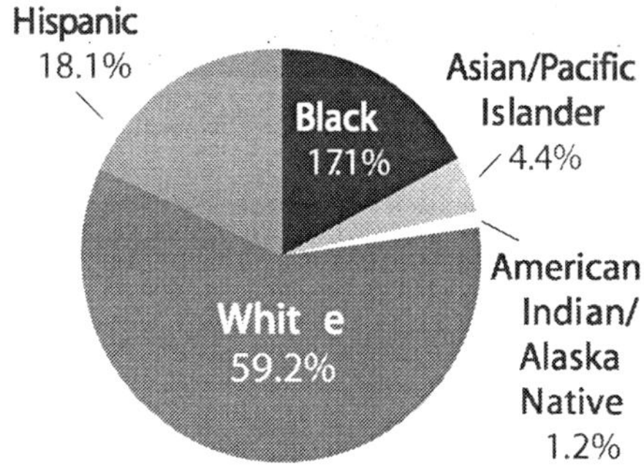

For the 1999-2000 school year, approximately 75 percent of all public school teachers were female.[15]

The average student : teacher ratio in 2002-03 was 16:1.[16]

The School Community

Teachers and Principals

The ratio of administrative staff members to teaching staff members is about even. Just over half (51 percent) of public school staff members are teachers.[17]

School principals are well-educated and experienced. Only around 10 percent of public school principals are under age 40, and 98 percent have a master's degree or above. About 44 percent of public school principals are women.[18]

Students

The majority of American public school students, 52 percent, attend suburban schools. Thirty-one percent of public school students attend city schools, and 17 percent attend rural schools.[19]

School Districts

- The 100 largest public school districts account for less than 1 percent of districts, but they also account for 22 percent of students and 16 percent of schools.[20]
- The two largest public school districts are New York City Public Schools and the Los Angeles Unified School District. These districts are each larger than over half of the individual state education systems.[21]
- The states with the largest percentage of minority students are California, Hawaii, Louisiana, Mississippi, New Mexico, and Texas. In addition, the District of Columbia reports 95.7 percent minority students.[22]

Graduation Trends

More Americans have completed high school.

- Between 1990 and 2003, the proportion of the adult population 25 years of age and over who had completed high school rose from 78 percent to an all-time high of 85 percent. [23]

Bachelor's degrees are becoming more common

- Between 1990 and 2003, the proportion of the adult population 25 years of age and over with a bachelor's degree increased from 21 percent to an all-time high of 27 percent.[24]

College financial aid is on the rise.

- Under the president's 2005 budget request, overall student financial aid would grow to $73.1 billion.[25]
- The number of recipients of grant, loan, and work-study assistance would increase by 426,000 to 10 million students and parents.

NATIONAL EXPENDITURES AND ACHIEVEMENT

As a nation, we now spend $501.3 billion annually at all levels of government on elementary and secondary education.

American taxpayers invest more in education than in the Defense Department. The United States invests more per pupil than almost any other nation in the world. Unfortunately, as Organization for Economic Development Education Director Barry McGaw noted, "The U.S. doesn't get the bang for its buck."

Expenditures for Elementary and Secondary Education [26]

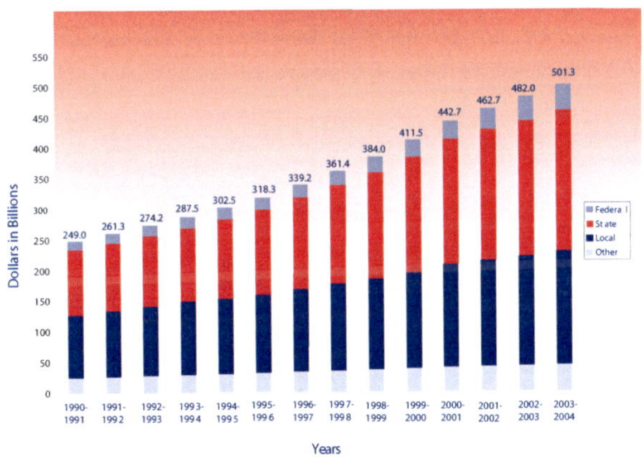

Much work remains to close the achievement gap in the early years. Even after four years of public schooling, most students perform below proficiency in both reading and mathematics. Minority and disadvantaged students are most at risk for falling behind.

4th-Grade Reading Proficiency: 2003 [27]

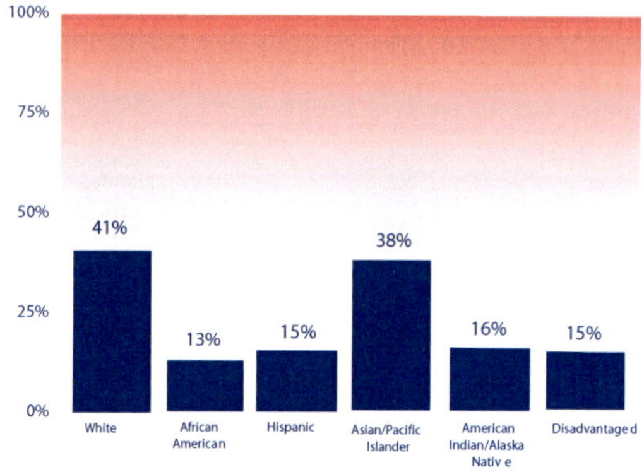

4th-Grade Math Proficiency: 2003 [28]

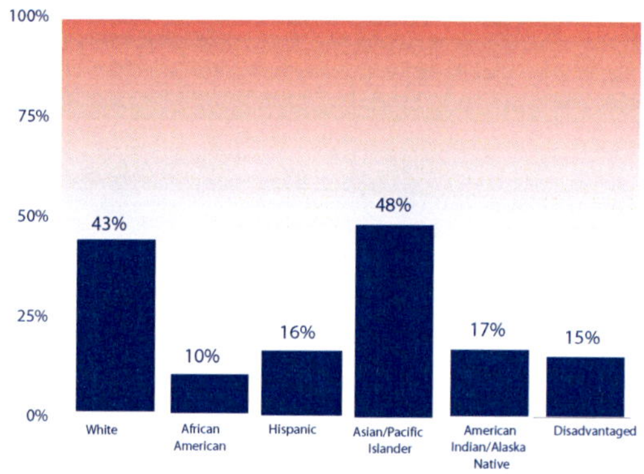

Upon graduating from high school, few students have acquired the math and science skills necessary to compete in the knowledge based economy.

12th-Grade Math Proficiency: 2000 [29]

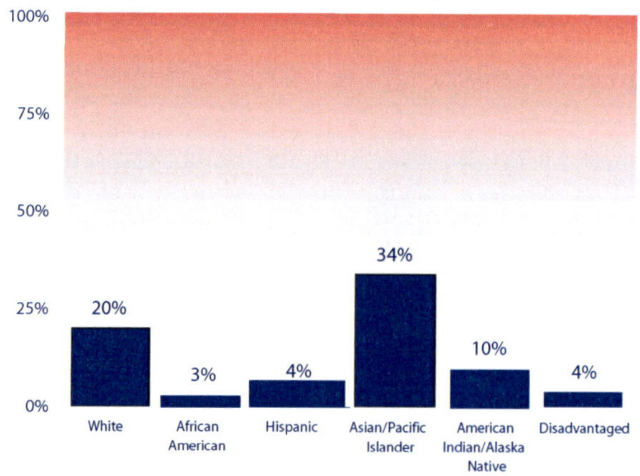

12th-Grade Science Proficiency: 2000 [30]

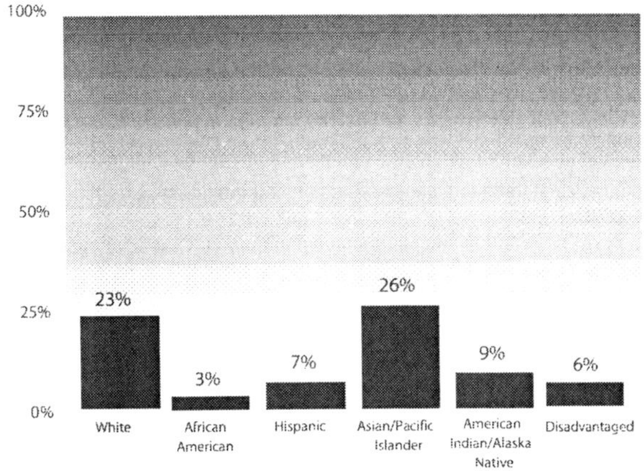

The principles of *No Child Left Behind* date back to *Brown v. Board of Education*, when the U.S. Supreme Court outlawed racial segregation in public schools and determined that the "separate but equal doctrine" was unconstitutional. That decision is now 50 years old.

Just after the passage of the *Civil Rights Act* in 1964, the *Elementary and Secondary Education Act* became law in 1965. *No Child Left Behind* is the 21st-century iteration of this first major federal foray into education policy—a realm that is still mainly a state and local function, as envisioned by our Founding Fathers.

On Jan. 8, 2002, President Bush signed the *No Child Left Behind Act of 2001* (P.L. 107-110) into law with overwhelming bipartisan support. The final votes were 87-10 in the Senate and 381-41 in the House. Senators Ted Kennedy (D-MA) and Judd Gregg (R-NH) and Congressmen George Miller (D-CA) and John Boehner (R-OH) were its chief sponsors in the Senate and the House.

No Child Left Behind ensures accountability and flexibility as well as increased federal support for education. *No Child Left Behind* continues the legacy of the *Brown v. Board* decision by creating an education system that is more inclusive, responsive, and fair.

IMPROVING THE ACADEMIC ACHIEVEMENT OF THE ECONOMICALLY DISADVANTAGED

The flagship federal education program, known as the "Title I" program, provides supplemental education support for students who are eligible for free or reduced-price lunches in school.

The program serves more than 15 million students in nearly all school districts and more than half of all public schools, including two-thirds of the nation's elementary schools.

Too often, these students do not receive the educational foundation they need to achieve their full potential in school or in life.

Support: Title I program funding increases to $13.3 billion for students in high poverty schools under the president's 2005 budget request. The president requested his third consecutive increase of $1 billion for disadvantaged students, or 52 percent over 2001 funding.

Preparing, Training, and Recruiting Highly Qualified Teachers and Principals

Under *No Child Left Behind*, all teachers must be highly qualified by the end of the 2005-06 school year. One of the most important ways to close the achievement gap and provide all children with a great education is to provide them great teachers. Studies have shown the single greatest effect on student achievement is teacher quality. For this reason, America must remain steadfast in meeting the goal of ensuring that every classroom has a highly qualified teacher.

To be "highly qualified," a teacher must (1) hold a bachelor's degree, (2) hold a certification or licensure to teach in the state of his or her employment, and (3) have proven knowledge of the subjects he or she teaches.

Support: Under the president's 2005 budget request, teachers receive $5.1 billion in support through training, recruitment incentives, loan forgiveness, and tax relief—up from $4.4 billion in 2004.

Language Instruction for Limited English Proficient and Immigrant Students

President Bush is committed to expanding educational opportunities for all students, including students who are learning the English language and students who are new to this country.

Children learning English face some of the greatest educational challenges due to language and cultural barriers. That is why President Bush and Congress pushed through the historic education reforms of *No Child Left Behind.* The law ensures that all children—from every ethnic and cultural background—receive a quality education and the chance to achieve their academic potential.

Support: The president's 2005 budget provides $681 million for English language acquisition funding for children who are learning the English language, so they can reach their academic potential and fully participate in the American dream.

Giving Parents Choices and Creating Innovative Education Programs

No child should be trapped in an underperforming school. Under *No Child Left Behind*, students who attend Title I schools that do not make adequate yearly progress, as defined by states, for two consecutive years have the option of transferring to a higher performing public school or a charter school within their district.

The promotion of charter schools is an important component of *No Child Left Behind.* These schools are held to the same accountability standards as traditional public schools, but they face fewer burdensome regulations. The result is more room for educators to be innovative and more choices for parents.

Support: Funding for choice and options for students and parents expands to $504 million under the president's 2005 budget request—an additional $113 million—to empower families to find schools that best meet the needs of their children, in particular those who need help the most.

MAKING THE EDUCATION SYSTEM ACCOUNTABLE

Accountability is a crucial step in addressing the achievement gaps that plague our nation. For too long, the poor achievement of our most vulnerable students has been lost in unrepresentative averages. African American, Hispanic, special education, limited English proficient, and many other students were left behind because schools were not held accountable for their individual progress. Now all students count.

Under *No Child Left Behind*, every state is required to 1) set standards for grade-level achievement and 2) develop a system to measure the progress of all students and subgroups of students in meeting those state determined grade-level standards.

Support: For fiscal year 2005, President Bush requested $410 million to support the development and implementation of state assessments to ensure students, parents, and teachers receive vital information about the performance of individual students, schools, and school districts.

MAKING THE SYSTEM RESPONSIVE TO LOCAL NEEDS

In addition to being accountable, states and school districts have the flexibility to pursue educational excellence by the means that best meet their needs. *No Child Left Behind* provides unprecedented levels of flexibility regarding the management of federal funds.

For example, most school districts may transfer up to 50 percent of the funding they receive under four major formula grant programs (Teacher Quality State Grants, Educational Technology State Grants, Safe and Drug-Free Schools and Communities State Grants, and State Grants for Innovative Programs) to any one of these programs or to the Title I program for disadvantaged students.

HELPING ALL CHILDREN LEARN TO READ

Because President and Mrs. Bush know that reading is the foundation for all other learning, the administration has set the goal of making sure every child knows how to read at grade level by the third grade. Reading opens doors to children who otherwise would struggle through school, lacking the skills to succeed and grow. Literacy is a vital skill for a successful student.

Children who learn to read well early in life are more likely to be engaged in school and experience academic success. A deficiency in reading skills impacts achievement in all other areas of education.

Support: Under President Bush's latest budget request, reading funding increases to a total of $1.4 billion, including $1.1 billion for the Reading First program, $132 million for Early Reading First programs, and $100 million for the Striving Readers program to meet the president's goal of ensuring every child can read on grade level.

Helping Children With Disabilities

The Department of Education is committed to ensuring that all children — including children with disabilities — receive a high-quality education. Before the passage of *No Child Left Behind*, the 1997 reauthorization of the Individuals with Disabilities Education Act (IDEA) required that students with disabilities be included in state and district wide assessment programs. *No Child Left Behind* builds on this requirement by ensuring that these assessments measure how well students with disabilities have learned required material in reading and mathematics. Students with the most significant cognitive disabilities can have results from specially designed alternate assessments used in accountability decisions instead.

Support: Special Education Grants to States Program would receive a record $11.1 billion under the 2005 budget request. This represents the president's fourth consecutive request for a $1 billion increase to support children with disabilities—a 75 percent increase over the funding level when the president took office and the highest level of federal support ever requested for children with disabilities.

Terms To Know

Adequate Yearly Progress: Under *No Child Left Behind*, each state establishes a definition of "adequate yearly progress" (AYP) to use each year to determine the achievement of each school district and school. States are to identify for improvement any Title I school that does not meet the state's definition of adequate yearly progress for two consecutive years.

Participation Rate: In order to make "adequate yearly progress" (AYP), schools must demonstrate that at least 95 percent of all students participated in the state assessment at each grade. This requirement must be met for all students in a school and for subgroups of those students defined by race/ethnicity, poverty level, disability, and English language proficiency.

Disaggregation: To ensure that children who are performing poorly are not lost in averages of achievement results, each state must report the performance of various subgroups if the subgroup is large enough for statistical reliability as determined by the state.

Highly Qualified Teacher: To be deemed highly qualified, teachers must have: 1) a bachelor's degree, 2) full state certification or licensure, and 3) demonstrated competency in each subject they teach.

Demonstration of Competency: New elementary school teachers have to pass a state test on subject knowledge and teaching skills. Teachers in middle and high school must prove that they know the subjects they teach by passing a state test in their subjects, completing an academic major or coursework equivalent to a major in their subjects, or by receiving an advanced degree or advanced certification/credential. Experienced teachers may also prove competency through HOUSSE (see below).

High, Objective, Uniform State Standard of Evaluation (HOUSSE): NCLB allows states to develop an additional way for current teachers to demonstrate subject-matter competency and meet highly qualified teacher requirements. Proof may consist of a combination of teaching experience, professional development, and knowledge in the subject garnered over time in the profession.

U.S. Secretary of Education
Rod Paige

We should think big thoughts and have high expectations. The American school system must become and remain the best in the world. We need all of our students to excel, not just some. The president wants to raise all schools to the highest levels of scholarship and motivation. The essential first step is the *No Child Left Behind* law, because it makes education more inclusive, fair, and successful.

REFERENCES

[1] Employment Policy Foundation (2004). Data analysis of Current Population Surveys from March 1993 and March 2003, U.S. Department of Commerce, Bureau of the Census.

[2] Bureau of Labor Statistics, Bureau of the Census. 2003 Annual Averages. Unemployment rates for people ages 25 and over.

[3] The Teaching Commission (2004). *Teaching at Risk: A Call to Action.* New York: Author.

[4] U.S. Department of Education, National Center for Education Statistics. Unpublished tabulations compiled from Common Core of Data for 2002-03 School Year.

[5] U.S. Department of Education, National Center for Education Statistics. Unpublished tabulations compiled from Common Core of Data for 2002-03 School Year.

[6] U.S. Department of Education, National Center for Education Statistics. Unpublished tabulations compiled from Common Core of Data for 2002-03 School Year. Elementary schools are 26 schools beginning with grade 6 or below and with no grade higher than 8. Secondary schools are schools with no grade lower than 7.

[7] U.S. Department of Education, National Center for Education Statistics (2003). *A Brief Profile of America's Private Schools,* Table 1.

[8] Center for Education Reform (2004). *National Charter School Directory, 9th Edition.* Washington: CER Books.

[9] Center for Education Reform (2004). *National Charter School Directory, 9th Edition.* Washington: CER Books.

[10] U.S. Department of Education, National Center for Education Statistics (2004). "1.1 Million Home schooled Students in the United States in 2003," *Issue Brief.*

[11] U.S. Department of Education, National Center for Education Statistics. Unpublished tabulations compiled from Common Core of Data for 2002-03 School Year.

[12] U.S. Department of Education, National Center for Education Statistics. Unpublished tabulations compiled from Common Core of Data for 2002-03 School Year. 27

[13] U.S. Department of Education, National Center for Education Statistics (to be available soon). *Digest of Education Statistics 2003.*

[14] U.S. Department of Education, National Center for Education Statistics (2003). *Digest of Education Statistics 2002*, Table 68.

[15] U.S. Department of Education, National Center for Education Statistics (2003). *Digest of Education Statistics 2002*, Table 68.

[16] U.S. Department of Education, National Center for Education Statistics. Unpublished tabulations compiled from Common Core of Data for 2002-03 School Year.

[17] U.S. Department of Education, National Center for Education Statistics. Unpublished tabulations compiled from Common Core of Data for 2002-03 School Year. Numbers from the fall of 2002.

[18] U.S. Department of Education, National Center for Education Statistics (2003). *Digest of Education Statistics 2002*, Table 85. Numbers from 1999-2000 school year.

[19] U.S. Department of Education, National Center for Education Statistics. Unpublished tabulations compiled from Common Core of Data for 2002-03 School Year. 28

[20] U.S. Department of Education, National Center for Education Statistics. Unpublished tabulations compiled from Common Core of Data for 2002-03 School Year.

[21] U.S. Department of Education, National Center for Education Statistics. Unpublished tabulations compiled from Common Core of Data for 2002-03 School Year.

[22] U.S. Department of Education, National Center for Education Statistics. Unpublished tabulations compiled from Common Core of Data for 2002-03 School Year.

[23] U.S. Department of Commerce, Bureau of the Census (2004). 2003 Annual Social and Economic Supplement to the Current Population Survey; and March Current Population Surveys 1952-2002.

[24] U.S. Department of Commerce, Bureau of the Census (2004). 2003 Annual Social and Economic Supplement to the Current Population Survey; and March Current Population Surveys 1952-2002.

[25] All budget numbers from the Department of Education Fiscal Year 2005 Budget Summary.

[26] Chart provided by the U.S. Department of Education Budget Service. 29

[27] U.S. Department of Education, National Center for Education Statistics. National Assessment of Educational Progress, 2003 Reading Assessments. Disadvantaged defined by eligibility for free/reduced price lunch.

[28] U.S. Department of Education, National Center for Education Statistics. National Assessment of Educational Progress, 2003 Mathematics Assessments. Disadvantaged defined by eligibility for free/reduced-price lunch.

[29] U.S. Department of Education, National Center for Education Statistics. National Assessment of Educational Progress, 2000 Mathematics Assessments. Disadvantaged defined by eligibility for free/reduced-price lunch.

[30] U.S. Department of Education, National Center for Education Statistics. National Assessment of Educational Progress, 2000 Science Assessments. Disadvantaged defined by eligibility for free/reduced-price lunch.

INDEX

D

E

F

G

H

I

J

L

Q

R

S

T

U

V

W

Y